SHOEY
THE LIONHEART
THE MICK SHOEBOTTOM STORY

SHOEY
THE LIONHEART

THE MICK SHOEBOTTOM STORY

PHIL CAPLAN

TEMPUS

For Mick, who left a host of treasured memories, in the hope that he will remain one.

Front Cover: No stopping the blonde blur as he finds a gap in the Wigan defence at Headingley on 17 September 1966. *(Picture by Irvine Crawford)*

Back Cover: Mick Shoebottom resplendent in his club blazer.

First published 2004

Tempus Publishing Ltd
The Mill, Brimscombe Port
Stroud, Gloucestershire GL5 2QG
www.tempus-publishing.com

British Library Cataloguing in Publication Data.
A catalogue record for this book is available from the British Library.

ISBN 0 7524 3292 3

Typesetting and origination by Tempus Publishing.
Printed and bound in Great Britain

CONTENTS

FOREWORD

He was a god; a very, very special player. Whenever we used to clatter down that concrete ramp leading out of the dressing rooms on to the pitch at Headingley I used to think, 'Thank goodness he's on my side'. Tony Karalius always used to say that they had to push their stand-offs on at St Helens when they knew Mick was playing. We were fortunate because we'd got Mick Shoebottom – we thought whoever we played against would have to have someone absolutely outstanding to beat him. I was always glad when I knew he was coming out with me, especially at some of the more intimidating away venues like Hull, Widnes or Featherstone. In all the years I've played, there have only been a few players whom I felt that about. He was the first one.

He epitomized everything that was great about Rugby League, what it was all about and the qualities it has. He was a loveable rogue; as my wife got to know all the players at Leeds she said that they were the finest bunch of blokes you could ever come across. She was right, and Mick was top of the bunch. He never looked for trouble but was always stood next to you if there was any. I've never, ever known anybody enjoy something as much as Mick did when he played rugby; he laughed all the time, even if someone hurt him.

People are always saying to me, 'Don't you wish you played now?', and I always answer no. If I did then I wouldn't have played with Mick Shoebottom, and I feel so grateful and fortunate because that for me was the massive plus to being at Leeds at that time. I can't think of a higher accolade. We've laughed together, we've drunk together, we've got in trouble together, and I think a lot of us, because we were rugby players, hid the effect losing Mick had on us. We lost something that meant so much to us as a side and as individuals.

John Atkinson
Leeds, Yorkshire, England, Great Britain (1965-82)

When someone passes away everyone wants to say nice things about them but there's no over-emotion with this fellow just because he's not here – or even after he got injured – no sentimental elevating him to something he never was, Mick was just an outstanding player. Everyone wanted to pay tribute to him.

I don't like the word 'hate' but in a sporting context there were some villains playing in those days, and that was without the benefit of slow motion replays or the 'on report' system, but Mick was a hard player and the opposition used to hate coming up against him. Ask Roger Millward, Alan Hardisty, Keith Hepworth, Kenny Gill at Salford, David Watkins – who never won at Headingley, all the Lancashire lads, he was a handful around them. There were some big, tough, hard, fast, brilliant forwards around the pack in those days but Shoey, he could tackle – I've seen him lift props back from over the line – he had good hands, he could sidestep, he could run. He had a pale complexion, he wouldn't catch the sun, with blondish hair, and in the opening minutes of a game he'd start to work and begin to colour from the neck upwards. It was as if he was coming to the boil and after about ten minutes his whole face would be bright red as if he'd got steamed up, and then he'd be off. In today's game he would have been the perfect man, forty years too soon, bless him, but what a player!

I've been involved at Leeds for forty-two years and playing with lads like Shoey was the highlight for me, I was just so privileged to be involved with that team, to be in their company and be part of the fun. We always stuck together through thick and thin and at the end of it all, it's people who matter. He was a man's man, a player's player, supporters' favourite, and just a great bloke. He was never nasty; only ever over-exuberant and enthusiastic, a true great.

Alan Smith
Leeds, Yorkshire, England, Great Britain (1962-83)

MICK SHOEBOTTOM
AN APPRECIATION

Mick Shoebottom would have been sixty this year. Cruel circumstance robs us of his company to celebrate such a landmark but hopefully this book will allow those who knew him, saw him play or are intrigued by his story to remember and appreciate his deeds on the Rugby League field. Mick packed more into a tragically foreshortened career than the vast majority of sportsmen do in a lifetime, his ever-cheerful perseverance to overcome adversity on and off the field its own tribute to him. This commemoration is intended to be a portrait of the man, a snapshot of his endeavours, humour and character. It principally celebrates his career in the colours of Leeds, Yorkshire, England and Great Britain with additional background information to help provide an appreciation of the determination behind the impish smile.

The willingness and relish with which all of those who were asked to contribute to this essentially extended testimonial did so, says much about its subject. Every one of them was so enthusiastic to tell a tale or share a recollection, their eyes lighting up at the opportunity to provide a permanent reminder of someone they clearly held so dear. Common traits and qualities quickly began to emerge when they spoke so fondly of him; fearlessness, bravery, exuberance, bravado and, because of his contagious personality, the kind of comradeship that perhaps is only really understood within the inner sanctum of the dressing room.

Shoey, as everyone knew him, would not countenance defeat or even the thought that a side he was part of would be second best. Underdogs yes but psychologically beaten before a jersey was put on, never. When a picture was commissioned by Leeds to present to his relatives as a lasting memento of his time and special talents at the club, some debate went into what would be the most appropriate epithet but, inevitably, the choice was limited to one word, 'Lionheart'; the perfect description for his fervent approach to the toughest of team sports. Physically he gave height and weight away to many an opponent but because of the passion, desire and a seemingly inexhaustible spirit that came from within his slight frame, he seldom came off second best. Rugged, tenacious, unyielding, he was the kind of player team-mates were grateful for and opponents tried desperately, but invariably unsuccessfully, to avoid. An oft repeated modern-day phrase is that players 'put their bodies on the line' but that was Mick's stock-in-trade. His contemporaries recall a Boxing Day clash at his beloved Headingley against Castleford when Malcolm Reilly in his glorious pomp burst onto the ball in rampaging style and looked certain to score between the posts. Mick hit him front on and brought him crashing to the ground yards short, the try saved and with no thought to personal cost as both men were led dazed from the fray.

Although Mick clearly relished the rugged, defensive aspect of the game – appropriate for someone who graduated from an amateur club named Bison's Sports – there was so much more to his play than that. His talents were such that he could operate equally effectively in any of the back positions and occasionally at loose forward, for him it was never where he played, only that he did. Superb hands when whipping the ball away to one of the most potent backlines in the game's history, giving centres like Syd Hynes and Bernard Watson the space and time to unleash the finishing prowess of wingers John Atkinson and Alan Smith; he was also adept at spotting and exploiting the smallest of gaps around the play-the-ball area – attributes which might have made him a fearsome hooker in the modern era. His support play was exceptional, feeding off the precision, slipped passes of the likes of Mick Clark and Ray Batten before scampering away – usually in arcing run - to the whitewash, his Leeds ratio being a try every two and a half appearances. In fact, it is difficult to think of a weakness in his game.

In the 1970 Test series down under, the last time Great Britain held the Ashes, he responded to the Lions' injury crisis by turning out at full-back in the decider in Sydney, the Aussies smugly believing that he would be a brittle last line. The more they kicked to him, the further he ran the ball at them, continually putting them on to the back foot and setting up waves of counter-attacks which eventually led to a five-one try count and dramatic victory for the tourists. Domestically, he was peerless in Leeds sides which swept all before them in the late sixties and at the start of the seventies. Roy Francis' and Derek Turner's squads were incredibly fit and given licence to thrill but the players also knew that if they made a mistake it would almost certainly be Mick who bailed them out and got the bandwagon moving again. He picked up every major medal available to him in a fantastic career which lasted nine glorious seasons. The manner of its ending in 1971 remains one of the heartbreaking stories in Rugby League history. A fortnight away from his second Wembley appearance, he was tragically injured when scoring a typically rip-roaring try against Salford in the Championship play-offs. It mattered less that his infectious enthusiasm was lost to his colleagues once the seriousness of the impact became apparent and he struggled for his very life. Like so many of his on-field battles, he won through but at great cost.

I was fortunate enough to begin my Rugby League education at Headingley at a time when Mick and his cohorts were producing a stunning brand of breathtaking football which saw the blue and amber reign supreme. For an impressionable youngster, new to the sport, he epitomized everything a first real hero should be and left an indelible mark. It has been an absolute honour and delight to spend time with his contemporaries, who we watched with increasing awe then, remembering their deeds. None of this would have been possible without the support, backing and resources of Mick's brother George and his niece Vicky who helped make it as near an 'authorised' account as is possible without the great man to refer to. Hopefully their faith in the project has been justified.

Phil Caplan
October 2004

ACKNOWLEDGEMENTS

To T.C. for arranging the initial contact, George Shoebottom and Vicky Parkin for access to their indispensable resource materials, the Charmaks for allowing me to sift through their collection of memorabilia, Ray Fletcher for his ever-assiduous checking of statistics and Peter Smith and Stuart Martel for their painstaking proofreading.

I am indebted and immensely grateful to the friends, team-mates and colleagues of Mick who allowed me to share their anecdotes, reminiscences, memories and, in particular, for their company, especially the irrepressible Harry Jepson OBE, and to Alan Smith and John Atkinson for their poignant foreword.

The vast majority of the pictures and other associated images included are taken from Mick's scrapbooks, and if any breach of copyright has occurred, it is entirely unintentional.

The game of Rugby League is continually appreciative of the support of Tempus Publishing for their willingness to chronicle all aspects of the sport, most especially James Howarth, Holly Bennion and Emily Pearce.

Shoey – no prouder player carried the Leeds badge.

1

THE COSTLIEST TRY

The initial worry was would he be all right for Wembley? It might only be Leigh, the longest priced outsiders in Challenge Cup Final history, but Leeds could ill-afford to be without their galvanizing, tenacious half-back. The try was typical Shoey; three Salford defenders – including international full-back Paul Charlton – left clutching in his wake as he powered onto Bill Ramsey's pass and made the whitewash at the corner before covering loose forward Colin Dixon belatedly clattered into the side of his head as he began to roll over. Mick's beloved Headingley fell momentarily silent, engulfed by a collective intake of breath, their cheers turned into instant concern as their seemingly indestructible hero was escorted, dazed and bewildered, away from the action by physiotherapist Eric Lewis and coach Derek Turner. That alone was an ominous sign; he was rarely forced from the field of play and although the initial diagnosis was confirmed as a broken jaw and severe concussion, it soon became clear that any battle to be fit for the game he so manifestly loved was to be superceded by a greater fight for life itself.

Initially he was carried to the touchline, but was quickly on a stretcher on his way back to the dressing room as Barry Seabourne sent Bob Haigh in for a try to make it 19-2 after half an hour of the second round Championship play-off clash. By the time the match was over, Leeds running out easy winners, Shoey was on his way to the General Infirmary where early the following week the extent of his injury began to emerge. Initially it had been hoped that he would still be fit to take his place in the Cup Final but Leeds Football Chairman Jack Myerscough read a statement after visiting his star man which said, 'The doctor had a full consultation with the specialist this morning. Shoebottom has not yet recovered from the effects of his concussion. He also has an undisplaced fracture of the lower jaw and will be wearing a dental harness for three weeks.'

Mick never played again, forced into premature retirement at the age of twenty-six on 1 May 1971 after 288 appearances for Leeds and twelve for his country, his dynamic talent and swashbuckling bravado lost at its peak. Seven winner's medals in four glorious seasons in the late '60s and early '70s as first Roy Francis' and then Derek Turner's sides revolutionized the way Rugby League was played, were fitting tribute to his constant determination and zealous enthusiasm, but what might have been? His all-action style and commitment made him an instant fans' favourite, his enormous zest for the code such that he once said, 'I'd play twice every day if I got the choice', but more than that his selflessness in battle made him a true players' player.

The fateful moment on Saturday 1 May 1971, at around 3.25 p.m. Seconds later Mick's career was over.

Concerned Leeds coach Derek Turner and physiotherapist Eric Lewis carry a stricken Shoey to the touchline in what was to be his final appearance.

In January the following year Leeds entertained Great Britain in aid of his hastily-arranged testimonial and the regard with which he was held is amply illustrated by the comments of his fellow professionals who paid tribute to him in the accompanying match programme. 'Rocky' Turner, one of the hardest men ever to lace a boot, who played and coached against Shoey before becoming his overseer, noted, 'I have met a lot of players in my time but I do not know of one I would have exchanged for Mick Shoebottom. His spirit was amazing, his courage magnificent – a player who would give all he had for his team in every match.' His skipper at Leeds at the start of that glory run and fellow Lions tourist, prop Mick Clark, stated, 'The finest rugby player I ever came across, Mick's rare ability put his mark on every match. He had a great sense of humour; he inspired his team-mates on the field and was liked by all of them.' One of his greatest adversaries, impish St Helens, Warrington, Leigh, Lancashire and Great Britain half-back Alex Murphy added, 'When people talk about professionals, Mick Shoebottom was the perfect example of a Rugby League player. His courage and ability will be missed…He was a wonderful club man for Leeds.' Headingley scout and erstwhile coach Joe Warham paid his tribute, 'Probably the best all-round player I signed was Mick Shoebottom. He was great on attack and in defence. I believe he would have gone on to even greater things but for his tragic injury. Every possible peak was scaled, world renown achieved and universal acclaim was accorded him. Yet the person himself was completely unspoiled.

Whether leading the team coach in song, bidding furiously at cards or cracking pre-match jokes, the same bubbling enthusiasm drove him to the forefront. His play, skilful as it was, showed the same lack of sophistication. On the field or off he was the cheerful, uncomplicated extrovert. He was a man who struck fear and respect into the opposition; he hadn't an enemy in the world. He was every man's man.' He was also one of the most versatile, achieving glories for club and country in a number of positions and, significantly, was always prepared to put the welfare of the team above his own.

Although in obvious discomfort, he appeared a fortnight after the incident with the side on the steps of Leeds Town Hall and spoke to the assembled crowd, who gave him a rousing ovation, as the City Council gave the Loiners a Civic Reception in recognition of their feat of winning the Yorkshire Cup and Floodlit Trophy that season, and despite ignominious defeat at the Twin Towers to a Murphy-inspired Leigh. It was one of the biggest upsets in Cup history with Leeds' skipper and one of Mick's closest friends Syd Hynes, who had come up with him through the Hunslet Schools' ranks, the first man to be dismissed at the Wembley showpiece. Ironically, Shoey's desperate efforts in the success over Salford – which ensured Leeds played St Helens in the Championship semi-final the following week – meant that Hynes was cleared to play in the Cup showdown after serving a two match suspension. Disenchanted and disconsolate Leeds fans could only wonder how it had all gone so dramatically and embarrassingly wrong in the capital in front of a nationwide audience, but esteemed *Yorkshire Evening Post* journalist Arthur Haddock in his analysis identified exactly where the problem lay. 'If the Leeds contingent had any doubt before regarding what made their team tick', he wrote, 'it cannot exist now. This 24-7 defeat at least showed that without midfield men Shoebottom and Batten they lose much of their efficiency. Batten's creative skill and the general industry of Shoebottom were sadly missed…there was no thrust from the engine room because the chief engineer and leading stoker were onlookers.'

Soon after, Shoey was re-admitted to hospital where the work of a dental surgeon was quickly superceded by that of a neurosurgeon after he suffered a stroke and the full extent of his injuries became known. The hospital and his wife Carol, a former orthopaedic nurse who he had met when being treated for an earlier back injury in Pinderfields Hospital in Wakefield, were inundated with messages of support from throughout the Rugby League community. He was buoyed and amused when a poll of female League supporters in the Yorkshire region voted him their number one pin-up in an attempt to find the code's top 'He-Man' but in all he was hospitalized for nine gruelling weeks with an initial prognosis that a full recovery would be, at best, extremely slow. Problems with his speech and memory, a loss of feeling down his complete right-hand side and a consequent initial change in his happy-go-lucky temperament borne out of frustration and a struggle to cope with the accompanying depression meant that his life would never be the same again. After his eventual release from the infirmary and a projected extensive period of rehabilitation, which included him having to re-learn to swim, an activity he had previously relished, newspaper headlines emblazoned the inevitable news that every Leeds fan dreaded to read, 'Shoebottom – the end'. His rugby career was over.

An Appeals Fund committee comprising of Leeds board member Noel Stockdale as chairman, directors Jack Myerscough, Fred Bartlett and Tim Healey, and general manager Alfred Rutherford, was hastily formed to look after Shoey's welfare after it was also revealed

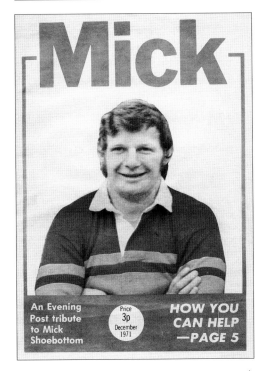

Above left: Front cover of the *Yorkshire Evening Post* tribute supplement.

Above right: Front cover of the hastily produced Testimonial Fund brochure.

that he would have to give up his job as a blacksmith at a local sign-writing firm, and this following the birth of his second child, Darren, just three weeks after his second admission. For Mr Stockdale there could be no worthier cause. 'Mick was more than a footballer. He had great moral stature which endeared him to all on and off the field. After one of the most serious injuries in the history of Rugby League, his courage helped the surgeons to win his battle for survival.'

A £5,000 donation from the club launched the benefit with Yorkshire Post Newspapers swelling the coffers by a further £250 'in recognition of Mick's wholehearted contribution to sport in the city'. They also brought out a sixteen page tribute supplement tracing his glittering career in which he helped guide Leeds to all the major trophies in the game. In it Arthur Haddock, who witnessed almost every one of his performances in blue and amber, paid fulsome praise; 'I always found him approachable, disarmingly frank and agreeably helpful', he wrote. 'Mick's was a great career … He was not the most artistic player who graced Rugby League, but he certainly figured among those who unfailingly gave 100 per cent loyalty, effort and determination, coupled with the ability to play in a number of positions. Mick was the type of player a manager loves to have. So long as he was playing, that was enough. I have known a lot of players in my time, but I never came across a harder grafter than Mick Shoebottom. He was still going when some of the others had had enough. Right from the start he would tackle anything in sight and such was his zest for work that the fans often said of him that as well as making his contribution to what the backs achieved he was "as good as a seventh forward". I once called him "the finest work-horse" of his time and this description remains the most apt I can conjure up. Mick, a dynamo on the rugby field, has always been an easygoing, modest, likeable lad off it. Certainly there never was any question, as with some players, of having to coax him into the training sessions; on the contrary it was difficult stopping him becoming over-trained.'

The Leeds Supporters' Club began their fundraising projects with a collection during the New Year's Day 1972 fixture against Wigan, generating the substantial sum of £567, and nominating him as their first player life-member. Highly-respected Yorkshire Secretary George Hirst summed up the feelings of many. 'His infectious enthusiasm and rich sense of humour from flashing eyes radiated to friend and foe alike. He holds, earned and deserved every honour the Rugby League could bestow upon one of its players. One could always truthfully say to him or of him, at the end of a game, "well done, lad, you've done your best".

Only Colin Dixon, who, like Shoey, died desperately prematurely, will know if there was intent behind their collision, but few blue and amber fans who witnessed the clash can be convinced otherwise. Their view is understandably echoed by Mick's elder brother George, who had introduced him to the sport. 'I'm convinced that the incident that not only ended his career but in many ways his life, because he suffered terribly after that, was deliberate, and I think the picture of it bears that out. The referee, Mr Hunt, had already given the try and turned away for the conversion when Dixon collided with him; he had no need to touch him, he could have stopped or jumped over him. The hospital would never commit themselves as to whether the brain cancer that eventually killed Mick could be traced back to that day but anyone with the slightest knowledge of the game knows that Dixon didn't have to do what he did; he could have jumped over him. He was nearly under the sticks on the dead ball line when Mick scored; there was no need for it. As to why, we will never know. Maybe some of it was down to Leeds being in the Challenge Cup Final. Players who weren't going always used to say to those who were "so you think you're playing at Wembley do you?" in the run up, it was always a test.'

Those on the field have a different view to those who looked helplessly on from the stands. Fellow professionals find it impossible to condemn one of their own men, despite the tragic consequences. Leeds scrum-half Barry Seabourne, who formed an almost irresistible partnership with Shoey during those glory years for the club says, 'None of the players had a really good view of what happened, Mick was haring for the corner and dived over and was rolling clear having put the ball down when the collision occurred. Colin Dixon was a great cover tackler and that was his job, to get across. I honestly don't know if he was just trying to jump over Mick.' Alan Smith, who came through the ranks with Mick and shared many of the great times with him for club and country, agrees. 'There isn't a player playing who would want to finish another's career, I cannot see that. I can't believe in my heart of hearts that Colin would want to do anything deliberately. Shoey never held any bitterness towards him when they met up later.' Fellow winger John Atkinson, who formed arguably the finest pairing in Leeds' illustrious history with Smith and twice toured with Mick is equally certain.

Opposite: Brochure cover for the Rugby League Film Night, held in aid of the Mick Shoebottom Fund.

RUGBY LEAGUE FILM NIGHT

Wednesday, 19th January 1972
Queens Hotel, Leeds
(In Aid of the Mick Shoebottom
Fund) **Presented by**

EDDIE WARING

BBC TV & Sunday
Mirror Columnist

Programme Free
**Donations
Accepted**

**SOUVENIR
PROGRAMME**

'I was on the far side to where the incident occurred so I didn't see it, but I went on a World Cup and an Ashes tour with Colin and a nicer man you couldn't wish to meet. Mick lived by the sword – that was how he played, he led with his head and he was the first to accept that it was just the consequence of playing rugby. Nobody will ever convince me that Colin kicked him with any intention. I knew him too well, had too much respect for him and liked him too much. I just couldn't imagine it, and it was alien to what Leeds and Salford matches were like, we had some fantastic free-flowing encounters.'

Every time Dixon appeared against Leeds after that, the home crowd left the 1974 Lions tourist in no doubt as to their opinion of his culpability in ending the career of their idol. Six months after the incident Dixon returned to Headingley to play in a League match and protested his innocence after being rounded on by the agitated home crowd, fuelled by the sight of Mick walking down the main stand touchline to sit next to Derek Turner to watch the action unfold. 'Immediately I ran on the field I was booed.' Dixon said in the aftermath. 'But I did nothing wrong the day Shoebottom was hurt. No one is sorrier than I that it happened. But it is not very nice to find everything blowing up in your face. It will not break me or cause me to give up Rugby League. I have nothing on my conscience.' The reported comments made by his wife Anne were hardly likely to diffuse the situation when, in supporting her husband, she added. 'It would have been better if the crowd had not seen Shoebottom before the match. We were so surprised…because we had almost forgotten the match in May.' The incidents also sparked off a war of words between the clubs, Salford Chairman Brian Snape refusing the hospitality of the Leeds directors and stating 'No Leeds official did anything to ease the tension in a nasty situation. They could have at least made a half-time announcement.' In response, Jack Myerscough defended the home club and their fans. 'The booing was just the crowd showing its feelings. Surely they have a right to do this. The medical authorities asked us to keep Shoebottom in the environment he had been used to, to try and help in his full recovery. That is why he watched the match from the touchline – a normal procedure.' George Shoebottom, however, thinks that the decision was insensitive and heightened an already volatile and emotional situation. 'One thing I didn't agree with, though, was Leeds' decision to parade Mick along the touchline the next time they played Salford. I can understand why they did it but it was always going to provoke and inflame the situation.'

Although sadly ending in tragedy, Shoey's was a career that an impressionable youngster from just off Low Road in Hunslet, born on Christmas Eve as war was starting to come to an end, could barely dream of.

2

A HUNSLET GROUNDING

Mick lived with his mother, Kathleen, in the family home in Spring Grove, Hunslet. He never met his father, George, a highly regarded bomb-disposal expert in the British Army. Whilst travelling back to Leeds to be with his wife, who was then pregnant with Mick, their fourth child, George was rushed from the train at Norwich station in an emergency to attend an unexploded bomb found at the Ipswich Infirmary. It went off while he was attempting to diffuse it. Such courage and fearlessness was mirrored each time Mick donned a rugby shirt, and it is likely that a measure of his determination also came from that source, as Mick's niece Vicky Parkin recalls. 'As the eldest niece, I spent a lot of time up at my Nanna's with Mick and his mum, and although she rarely talked about her marriage, she used to say that she and my grandfather adored each other. The only story she ever told me was that when he was forced to swim across a river in France to escape pursuing German forces, the only thing that kept him going was a vision he had of her face on the bank at the other side. I have no idea as to how Mick came to be given the second name of Dion, or if it was after someone, but such a choice definitely fits in with Kathleen's character and spirit.'

Mick was the youngest, behind his brother George, who was fourteen years his senior, and twin sisters Beryl and Myrna. In an area that has been extensively chronicled by the likes of Richard Hoggart, Keith Waterhouse and John Morgan, sport was a key element that bound the industrial working-class back-to-back community south of the River Aire together and Mick naturally gravitated to be a part of it. Ken Eyre, who was hewn of the same stone and was later to play alongside and keep a paternal eye on Shoey, feels that to understand the man you have to examine his roots, 'Mick, like a lot of his contemporaries, was born with no special privileges, but the thing that set Hunslet people apart, especially kids, was that sense of togetherness. Because you were of the same ilk you developed life-long friendships. All the kids loved all sports, my younger brother Albert was a schoolboy boxing champion; and all we did in summer was play cricket. If Mick was seen playing football it was only because he had a natural talent for the ball, whether it was round or oval. Even then I knew he was a sportsman because he could turn his hand to anything. The way rugby was organized then doesn't happen now. There were no structured teams for youngsters with qualified coaches at their side instructing them and a proper marked-out field. If you wanted to play rugby after school or at weekends on the Moor or the Plevna you had to play with the big lads because there was only one game going on. Mick, like everyone else, learnt his trade that way because

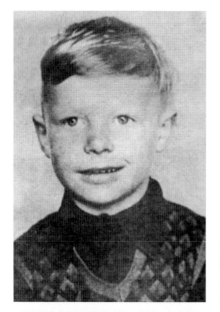

Mick at the age of five, at school aged eight, and at thirteen with brother George; treasured pictures from the family album.

there was merely a pitch with a game going on and as people arrived they just joined in on either side. If you were a youngster like Mick then you'd be stuck out on the wing or maybe at full-back but you were expected to hold your own against the big lads. It wasn't even a question of ability; if you wanted to play in the area then you were in with the older ones. That was the important factor in his development; he was growing up quickly in a big man's game.'

Mick's versatility was becoming increasingly well known, he was selected for the Leeds Schoolboys side at soccer and was a junior champion of boy's club diving, but rugby, for all its involvement and physicality, was easily his first love. It was a time Barry Seabourne recalls with obvious affection. 'All the schools in the Hunslet area used to play rugby so we were always coming into contact with each other even though we were different age groups. We all started playing for our schools around the age of eight and when there were fixtures on the Pepper Road playing fields or the Middleton clearing they would be like festivals, the Under-11s would play first followed by the other years up to the Under-15s. We all followed Hunslet in those days; we were always hanging around Parkside or playing together on a night up on the Moor. The area was just such an incredible production line for talent. It was always rugby in the winter and cricket in the summer and Mick was pretty good at both. Even though he was small, you could see then that he was honest and good-hearted.'

At the age of nine Mick gained selection in the Low Road School team and came to the attention of Harry Jepson. 'He was very different in playing style to his brother George, who I'd initially registered for Hunslet Schools; George was very angular, the opposite of Michael. Low Road was a good school for producing rugby players and one of his teachers was Idwal Davies, the Welsh Rugby Union centre who was a very good player and signed for Leeds just before the war, only for a bad shoulder injury to end his career early. I taught there for a short while with him while Shoey was just a little kid, a very small boy, almost slight. He started at Low Road as an infant and that was his only school until he left just before his birthday in 1958. He was a real tearaway as a youngster, full of mischief, not a thug or anything like that, just bouncing with energy. There were nineteen schools in Hunslet and all but one of them, Hunslet Moor which had a master who favoured soccer, played rugby. Apart from the few junior schools, they all had three teams; Under-11s, -13s and -15s so there was a lot of rugby being played and an obvious progression for the boys. The secret of our success, despite being the smallest district, was that because it was such a tight community, everybody knew each other and who the best up-and-coming players were. I first saw Mick play when he was in the senior team at Low Road where stalwarts of schools' rugby like Eric Rose and Frank Settle were in charge. His first 'city' game for Hunslet was away in Cumberland, as even though they were a county side by then they weren't strong enough to compete with Yorkshire and Lancashire schools. They dropped out of the County Championship in the mid-'50s, which was a pity because there was still a lot of great talent up there. I was secretary of the Hunslet Schools Association at that time and we had just retained the Yorkshire Shield for the second year and along with Chairman Joe Harold we decided to reward the lads initially with a tour up there. It then became a prestigious regular alternate fixture which carried a civic reception, the bulk of the council members being big Rugby League fans. By 1958, Hunslet Schools had gone four years without defeat in Yorkshire and Michael couldn't get into the team – which was brimming with talent including Syd Hynes and Albert Eyre at centre – because of his size for a stand-off. When we went up to Whitehaven that year we decided to have a look at one or two lads on the fringes, and he formed a partnership with Syd who was at scrum-half. Shoey may have been "a little 'un" but you could see as he trotted out onto the pitch that he felt ten feet tall. We were drawing 0-0 at half-time, principally due to the efforts of a Cumbrian referee, but we played downhill in the second half and ran out 22-0 winners. He played one other game for the city team before Christmas after that but then he left school, as part of the intake did in those days, and went to play for the Hunslet Boys Club rather than Hunslet Parkside, where most of the boys went whilst hoping to get noticed for the professional ranks.'

It was around that time that Ken Eyre, who had already struck up a firm friendship with Mick's brother, first saw the youngster in action. 'I came across him when he was playing for the City Boys side and I went to watch Albert in that team which included the likes of Barry Lee who later turned professional with Hunslet, and Billy Hood who was captain of the side. Mick's size was never really an issue as all of them were small, Syd Hynes and Barry Seabourne included, but he just had to be involved. Harry Jepson wasn't just the secretary of the schools rugby, he was also heavily involved at Hunslet, so he knew about any boy that showed any talent at school or came through that system, and you could guarantee he would be whispering in their ear that when they left school they should head down to Parkside. For whatever reason, Mick went to the Boys Club instead maybe because he wasn't given that much encouragement initially because of doubts over his size.'

Syd Hynes has fond memories of their initial partnership. 'We go back to schoolboy days, we played against each other and then together for the Hunslet City Boys team, I was at seven and he was playing six. He was like me; we were both very tiny as fourteen- or fifteen-year-olds, and we made our debuts together in Cumbria, which was frightening and incredibly exciting at the same time. I don't think either of us thought that we would be anything special at that time, but a few years later we played together again at Leeds and as soon as we renewed our partnership it was like nothing had changed.'

One of the earliest indications of Mick's courage came after leaving school when he severely broke an ankle playing for the Boys Club. It was an injury which, especially in those days, would have ended thoughts of ever playing top level sport for a lesser character. Mick's brother George recalls, 'His foot was turned right round and facing the wrong way. Jack Hirst, who was a well-known local teacher and stalwart of the club, carried him off. It took a long time to heal and was always a potential weakness afterwards but he must have worked on his upper body because when he came back into amateur football, he had put all his top weight on.' Mick was out of the game he by now so passionately loved for fourteen torpid months. Painstakingly he not only worked himself back to fitness but, combined with a growth spurt, developed his physique predominantly through obsessive cycling. Using a second-hand bike which his mother bought for him, he punished himself on rides throughout the county to continually exercise and strengthen the ankle and build up his general stamina. Stories claim that when Kathleen asked him where he was going when he got the rusty two-wheeler out, he would reply 'Scarborough' and he very possibly meant it.

All the while Shoey remained in and around Rugby League, usually following George, and as soon as he could he was back playing. 'He joined what I always called the "big boys game" with me at Coughlans, based around the forge, who won the Leeds and District Cup', George recounts, before adding the startling revelation that Mick was not quite the one-club man that history indicates. 'He came down to train with us and get with the lads and used to watch us play, he must have been about fifteen at the time. I then got taken on at Hull K.R. for a short spell until Colin Hutton, who was later to coach Mick in the international arena, took over and got rid of the dead wood – of which I was one. From there I went to Doncaster and really enjoyed it. Every so often I used to take Mick with me to Tattersfield and he actually played one first team game for them as 'A.N. Other' on or around his sixteenth birthday. They always paid the players about three months late but the camaraderie down there was so good that we all used to put up with it. When I finished I went back to the amateur game in the Hunslet area.

The Hunslet City Boys team that travelled to Cumberland in 1957/58. From left to right, back row: Henderson, Dominichini, Lee, Harry Jepson (secretary), Eyre, Naylor, Jameson. Front row: Oglethorpe, Fannon, Mr D. Lewty (selection and training committee), Hood (captain), Mr W.J. Arnold (chairman), Hargreaves, Booth. Seated: Shoebottom and Hynes.

I trained with Bison's but they wouldn't let me play for them because I wasn't an employee. Instead I lined-up against them for Coghlans on what we used to call 'the nettle pitch' and I scored the first try down there, and from then on they said I could join them. Mick was already working there so we teamed up together and that's what I really class as his beginning.'

Once back and regularly involved, it did not take Mick long to return to full fitness, as George quickly found out. 'We were at an annual sports day that Bison's used to hold like a lot of firms in the area, and we were on different teams – he would have been about sixteen and I was thirty. It was a really good day with every event going, ending with the relay. Mick came up to me and asked which number I was going, I told him last man and he just said "oh right" and went back to his mates. I was 10 yards in the lead for my team when I got the baton and I could hear the watching crowd roaring "go on then Shoey", and I remember thinking "I'm great" and pushing my chest out just before Mick shot by me – it was him they were cheering, he could run. We all won a load of prizes between us that day but when we stood at the bus stop waiting to go home, Mick had twice as many as anyone else.'

In his last full season with Hunslet Boys Club, Mick kicked at least one goal in every match and before long he was an integral part of the Bison's side in the Leeds and District Amateur League, and in such company, Harry Jepson began to see the spark of what was to come. 'I never had doubts about his ability or desire, only his size, but when I went to see him play at Bison's he had really shot up physically and I couldn't believe it was the same boy. Mind you, working with the likes of Alan Preece and Cliff Williams in the building yard certainly made a difference.' Ken Eyre never had any doubts that Mick would make his way in the

Mick and elder brother George, anchors of the Bison's Sports side of the early 1960s, in the Leeds and District Amateur League. From left to right, back row: M. Priestman, N. Johnstone, P. Smalley, M. Pethrick, H. Britten, P. Tebbutt, D. Simpson, E. Wright, T. Garside. Front row: D. Miller, M. Shoebottom, B. Tate, G. Shoebottom, E. Thomas.

game, especially as his survival instincts were being honed in the toughest of environments. 'Because of the three years or so he'd had playing against older mates there was no fear for him playing in an open-age game aged fifteen. That grounding with Coughlan's and then Bison's was, in my book, the hardest Rugby League that you could play. You were going to places like Lock Lane at Castleford and Dewsbury Celtic, they were all superb teams but hard-as-nails, there were some real bruisers amongst them and Shoey was eagerly taking them on.'

There were a number of disparate factors which eventually came together to produce the most successful, sustained spell of trophy gathering in the history of the Leeds Rugby League club; visionary administrators, revolutionary coaches, an outstanding crop of carefully nurtured junior talent that came through together, but there was also a key, indefinable ingredient that Ken Eyre asserts was vital to the mix. 'If you look at the 1968 Wembley line-up there were seven of us who had played for Hunslet Schools; Mick Clark, me, our Albert, Bill Ramsey, Syd Hynes, Shoey and Barry Seabourne – over half the side. We've never all sat down and discussed it but there has been the occasional banter about there being, say, three of us from Bewerley Street and one from Hunslet Carr, there's still that rivalry. What the lads who came from Hunslet brought was, maybe, something that was never at Leeds in any great strength, although it was always a terrific club. It was a spirit that can't really be explained or described, or something you can put your finger on. We don't have to see each other that often but when we do it's like we've never been apart. There was no "them" and "us" and that very quickly spread through the dressing room at Headingley. You got a team that could play football and a camaraderie that only those who were involved in it can truly understand. You've got to have certain abilities and the desire to work extremely hard, but his grounding also set Mick on the right road.'

3

IT COULD HAVE BEEN TRINITY

Mick began the 1961/62 Leeds and District Amateur season in sparkling style scoring nine tries in as many games and kicking goals in each of them. His dynamic form at Bison's was such that professional scouts were eagerly pursuing him as soon as he had celebrated his seventeenth birthday. Leeds had been keeping tabs on him from his schoolboy days but the first club to offer trials were Wakefield, Trinity taking him on for a month and handing him a Yorkshire Senior Competition debut against Hull Kingston Rovers in January 1962 at Belle Vue. Playing at scrum-half, he made an immediate impression and was labelled in the local press as '…a real find. A shrewd distributor of the ball, fast away from the scrum and a good defender, he seems destined to follow in the footsteps of the many famous scrum-halves who have worn the Trinity colours with distinction.'

Elder brother George naturally took it upon himself to look after any negotiations. 'Hunslet, Wakefield and Hull were all interested in Mick and Leeds just sat in the background. Colin Tomlinson, who had joined them from Bramley, had already told the Headingley management that he knew where there was a great up-and-coming lad – and that was our Shoey. He first went on trial to Wakefield and played three "A" team games. The last one, against Keighley, was abandoned because of fog and we were called in front of the full board at Belle Vue, which included football committee man John Simpson, the shoe shop owner in the city, and coach Ken Traill whom I knew from my playing days. Mr Simpson was insistent on one more trial, but I'd already said to Mick before we went in, "whatever I say you stand by" and he'd said okay. I'd already mentioned to him that he wasn't having another trial. I told the Wakefield board, "if you want him, he's there", and they asked us to leave the room, which we did. When we came back in they were still insisting on this extra match to decide, even though Ken had said to them if you don't sign him now then you're not going to get him, but the board insisted. We came home on the bus and Mick was terribly upset and was saying to me "I could have been…" but I told him "no because there might be something else in the pipeline".'

Wakefield legend Neil Fox knew that his club had made a mistake. 'Mick was always a very hard man to play against – especially in the tackle – but he never grumbled, no matter how hard a game might be or how much stick he had taken. I was at Wakefield when he played trial games with our "A" team and Trinity's players were very surprised when he did not join us.'

Trinity's prevarications were to come back and haunt them, and having been asked to be crossed off their register as an amateur, a chase began for Mick's signature between Hunslet, Keighley and Leeds. George, though, was already ahead of the game. 'Unbeknown to Mick I'd already had some feedback from Headingley who were checking on whether he had actually signed for Trinity. I told them he hadn't and they asked "does he want to play for Leeds?" and I said yes, even though Mick had no idea. They said bring him up tomorrow, and when I told Mick he couldn't really believe it and he duly signed. It was all done in double-quick time and there were only two men in the room, Arthur Clues and Alfred Rutherford, no ifs or buts, it was just done. They gave Mick a cheque and we came out and stood at the top of the steps and he whispered to me, "I could do with some money" because neither of us had any brass at the time, so I went back in and asked if he could have some of the fee in cash. Mr Rutherford took the cheque back and returned with a bundle of pound notes which Mick dropped all over the floor because he was so excited. That week Ken Traill went over to Bison's to see if it was too late to get him back to Trinity, that's how much he wanted him for Wakefield but the rest is history. Hunslet's policy at the time was to pay a £25 signing-on fee and then add "think of the glory". Alf Burnell was scouting for them then and he told the directors to give him £1,000 and he would do the deal but Mick was a schoolboy and they weren't prepared to pay such an amount and take a risk. A lot later Hunslet enquired about Mick but by then it would have cost them a minimum of £10,000 for someone they could have had for a few hundred quid.'

Mick initially signed alliance forms at Headingley, the minutes at the football committee on Monday 12 February 1962 recording perfunctorily, 'the Chairman stated that M. Shoebottom – scrum-half – had now been signed', and he was rushed into the 'A' team to play Castleford on the Saturday. With a blank weekend for the first team, he lined up in a side that contained a measure of experience, South African loose forward Louis Neumann resuming after being out for several weeks with a pulled hamstring, together with two local trialists. Alongside him for his historic first run out for the Loiners were: George Simpson, Michael Cadywold, Robin Dewhurst, A.N. Other (trialist), Eddie Ratcliffe, Trevor Oldroyd, Alan Jubb, Peter Umpleby, Alan Newbound, Colin Tomlinson, S.O. Else (trialist), Louis Neumann. Leeds won easily with Mick constantly involved and, after such a convincing performance, the Headingley management wasted little time in agreeing full terms. On the Monday, General Manager Alfred Rutherford wrote to him offering a contract which agreed to pay £600 for a relinquishing of his amateur status and although the exact total fee was not disclosed, it was reported that phased disbursements would rise to £1,200 according to the honours he may gain.

In that night's *Yorkshire Evening Post* a small block within the Rugby League news was titled 'Shoebottom signs' and by the end of the week his rise had reached fairytale proportions as he was named in the first team to face Doncaster partnering one of the legends of the code, the incomparable Lewis Jones. Arthur Haddock hinted towards the reason for Mick's rushed inclusion in his preview of the game in the *Yorkshire Evening News*: 'Overshadowing all else on the Rugby League front tomorrow', he wrote, 'is the top of the table clash of Wakefield and Wigan… Leeds, seeking to invest their home game with Doncaster with a spot of extra interest in view of the big Belle Vue attraction…are giving Mick Shoebottom his senior debut.' More to the point, the Loiners management were seeking a replacement for regular

19th February 1962.

Dear Mr. Shoebottom,

In consideration of your agreeing to abandon and relinquish the status of an amateur Rugby Football Player we hereby agree to pay you the sum of £600.

Yours sincerely,

[signature]

General Manager.

Signed *[signature]*

Yorkshire Senior Competition

A 'FIND' FOR TRINITY

Reserve scrum half impresses

Wakefield Trinity "A"
    (3g., 5t.) .... .. 21pts.
**Hull Kingston Rovers
    "A"** (2g., 1t.) .... 7pts.

In their first match this year at Belle Vue—they were last at home on November 25, 1961 — Trinity "A" scored a convincing success against the current leaders of the competition.

Aided by Kosanovic's astute hooking and clever open play, they were too fast and resourceful for the visitors, who had to do most of the chasing and tackling.

Shoebottom, from Bison's Sports made his debut for Wakefield at scrum half and on this showing is a real "find."

A shrewd distributor of the ball, fast away from the scrum and a good defender, he seems destined to follow in the footsteps of the many famous scrum halves who have worn the Trinity colours with distinction.

DEBUT FOR LEEDS

MICHAEL SHOEBOTTOM, the 17-year-old scrum-half, who makes his debut for Leeds against Doncaster at Headingley tomorrow.

Top: The beginning of a long and glorious career as Leeds offer terms to Mick after one 'A' team game.

Above: The Shoey legend begins.

Left: Despite a promising trial, Wakefield miss theiir chance to offer Mick terms.

scrum-half Colin Evans who had broken a big toe after dropping a vice on his foot whilst at work at Kirkstall Forge. As Leslie Temlett recorded in the *Yorkshire Evening Post*, 'The Leeds experiment against Doncaster is to bring into the first team – after one 'A' trial – following which he was signed, their new scrum-half recruit Mick Shoebottom, the former Bison's junior. The teenager was most impressive in his trial. Leeds feel he is sufficiently good for them to give Colin Evans, an ever present this term, a needed rest before the Leigh cup-tie.' There was further welcome news for Mick with a guiding hand re-called to play alongside him. 'The only other change is enforced through the suspension of Fred Pickup', continued Temlett. 'Colin Tomlinson takes his place with John Sykes going into the reserves.' Another eighteen-year-old, Robin Dewhurst, was drafted in on debut as full-back after Ken Thornett went down with flu just before kick-off, but it was Shoey who took the headlines. The reigning champions were always likely to complete the double over the lowly Dons and claim their seventh successive victory but it was the blooding of their latest talent that had the 6,516 fans drooling. He had already made a mark with his numerous bustling runs and shuddering tackles as the Loiners took an early 12-point first-half lead before his crowning glory. In the forty-third minute, Lewis Jones set the position by dummying his way to near the Doncaster line and when the ball was turned back on the inside Mick 'tore through a gap as wide as a house' to beat three defenders on a glorious charge to the posts, his dive over allowing him to join the celebrated band of players to score on their debut. A comprehensive, eight-try 34-8 victory was hardly unexpected but all of the reports focused on his dream start. 'Wakefield Trinity may some day regret the failure to snap up eighteen-year-old Mick Shoebottom, the Leeds League lad who slipped through their fingers', wrote one. 'Leeds stepped in to sign him and on the evidence of his debut against Doncaster believe they have done a shrewd stroke of business.' 'This likely looking customer had the Dons on the run several times, and marked much promising work with a picture try', exclaimed another. The *Yorkshire Post* paid the most fulsome tribute, 'Shoebottom reigned supreme round the scrums, tackled hard and sure, had the build to shake off tackles and the pace off the mark to take him through the gaps he so readily exploited.' It was a summation that could have been applied to the vast majority of his blue and amber performances over the next ten years. The teams for his historic bow were:

LEEDS: Robin Dewhurst, Garry Hemingway (two tries), Vince Hattee (one goal), Derek Hallas (two tries), Geoff Wrigglesworth (two tries), Lewis Jones (four goals), Mick Shoebottom (one try), Abe Terry, Barry Simms, Don Robinson (one try), Jack Fairbank, Colin Tomlinson, Brian Shaw.

DONCASTER: Price, Goodchild, Saville, Davies (one try), O'Neill, Dean, Doyle (one goal), Kirk, Heath, Goodyear, Hepworth, Wakefield (one try), Asquith.

Referee: Mr H.G. Hunt (Warrington).

His match fee was fourteen pounds, supplemented by 2/6d for expenses and with tax and contributions of £2, 7/4d deducted his eager exploits earned him £11 15/2d.

One person who was not surprised that Mick was an instant success was Hunslet prop Ken Eyre, later to join him at Headingley. 'I knew Michael's desire as a youngster would stand him in good stead and he was just one hell of a player. If you were picking a rugby team, and I don't care what era you're talking about, the first name I would put down on the team sheet no matter who you were up against would be Michael Shoebottom. People talk about the

The Leeds side that lost at Fartown, Huddersfield, in late 1962. Mick is on the far left of the front row with legendary skipper Lewis Jones crouching in the middle.

power he had for his size but he had so much ability and was a tremendous sight when in full flight running with his knees up. He was a totally dedicated rugby player, nothing fazed him, he didn't care who he was playing with or against he just got on with it. He could have signed with any number of clubs and being a Hunslet lad many of us thought that he should have come to Parkside with us but he went to Headingley and that was his stage. I always thought he was a natural stand-off, I saw opponents look at him with fear when I was putting my head into the scrum.'

It was to be almost two months before Mick made his second senior appearance, but he maintained his form with a series of impressive performances in a reserve side which heavily placed the accent on uncovering and developing young, local talent. Ken Eyre is certain that it was his tough upbringing in the local amateur game which gave him a start and an edge. 'It prepared him perfectly for second team rugby at Leeds which was a very hard, intensely physical game in those days. You had young guys coming up trying to impress and the older ones coming back who were basically slowing down and they just wanted to crack you and that basically was the nature of the game.'

Tries in impressive home wins over Batley 'A', York 'A' and Hull K.R. 'A' continued to build Mick's status amongst the discerning Leeds fans and he was selected to play against Wakefield in a midweek match rearranged from Boxing Day to early April, only for the game to be put back again. His eventual re-call came at Wilderspool on 14 April, his initial away game also bringing winning pay as Leeds hung on to triumph 13-8, and his first injury after he was knocked unconscious scrambling back in defence in an effort to prevent Dennis Glover scoring Warrington's sole try of a battling first half. Despite the blow, which yielded concussion, he typically came back to the bench after the break, ready to return in an emergency as the use of substitutes had not yet been introduced. When Eric Fraser made it only a 2-point margin between the sides with a penalty fifteen minutes from time and the match seemed to be slipping away from the Loiners, Mick returned on the left wing allowing Geoff Wrigglesworth to move inside to centre from where he scored the decisive try. Shoey also learnt another valuable lesson in his continuing education, being penalized in each of the first three Leeds scrums for feeding which caused referee Mr Wingfield to warn skipper Lewis Jones about his young partner's exploits.

With a staggering six games in eleven days to fit in around the Easter holidays to complete the league programme, the Leeds management was forced into judicious deployment of their resources and although Mick missed the comfortable home win over Hunslet on Good Friday, he was back in the side the following afternoon for another local derby against Bramley. The cloying mud as the result of incessant rain and the staging of a match less than twenty-four hours before restricted handling but Mick was in his element, chasing and harrying in defence and always looking to sweep the ball wide. The match was won by the Loiners in controversial fashion, former Villagers second-rower Colin Tomlinson snaring the winning try against his old club although many in the ground thought that he had been hauled down short of the line.

Six successive victories had given Leeds an outside chance of making the top four and the opportunity to defend the Championship crown they had joyously won for the first time the campaign before, but consecutive home defeats to Wakefield and Featherstone – Mick's fourth senior appearance – saw them miss out by just 2 points.

4

NOT A REGULAR YET

Having played four times for the first team in his debut season, Mick continued to serve his apprenticeship as an understudy to Colin Evans in an Alliance side that swept virtually all before it playing exciting, expansive rugby and building up a loyal and eager following. Their only defeat in the Yorkshire Rugby League Senior Competition Championship came disappointingly in the play-off final at home to Castleford when a crowd of over 2,000 saw them suffer their first setback of the season 21-5, Shoey grabbing the Loiners' sole touchdown. Some recompense came in the Yorkshire Senior Cup which saw him claim his first medal in the famous colours. Halifax were memorably beaten 9-3 in a tense second-round clash in front of 3,000 fans before Huddersfield were vanquished and Keighley tamed in the decider but only after a replay, 15-3, to give former Hunslet and Great Britain full-back Jack Evans' men deserved silverware. Billy Watts was starting to see the signs of what would later emerge. 'Mick was always so bubbly and on the bounce and even when he was in the reserves, the dressing room was always buzzing when he was there. When he arrived, like Harry Jepson said at the time, we all wondered whether he was going to be big enough but whatever he lacked in stature he more than made up in heart.'

Mick's stints on the main stage again coincided with the rigours of the holiday programmes, with three matches in early December and a further seven in late April and throughout May, after the season was extended following the notorious big freeze in 1963. Initially, a spectacular try, finished with a typically exuberant dive at the side of the posts, helped to polish off Swinton at Headingley in a match that saw second-rower Mick Joyce make his debut, but it was three months before Leeds were to play again at headquarters. That was unfortunate for Shoey as he had been initially drafted in to face the Lions after Evans suffered a fractured jaw at Oldham the week before. Reviews continued to be favourable, with the *Green Post* commenting, '...Joyce and Shoebottom have reached the point when they can be said to be knocking – and knocking hard – on the first team door.' Mick looked set for an extended run, and played in the sides which suffered consecutive defeats at St Helens and Huddersfield where Leeds failed to score a try, before the weather intervened. By now, though, he was starting to be recognized, John Atkinson being one of his early admirers. 'I watched Mick from the terraces play at scrum-half before he really blossomed into the stand-off we came to know, but the first time I saw him was in the café part of the bowling alley in the Arndale Centre in Headingley. He was having something to eat with

Left: The young Mick in pensive pose with a bright future beckoning.

Below: A gap-toothed Mick clearly relishing a training night at Headingley with Barry Seabourne on the extreme right.

Louis Neumann and the thing that immediately stood out about him was the size of his badge. It was a massive Leeds Rugby League crest which he used to get specially-made by Frank Child the tailors, and they were always a bit bigger than the club ones. In a way that summed him up where rugby was concerned, he was a larger than life character.'

Shoey was re-called as the Loiners faced a sapping spell of four games in five days over Easter, producing another sterling defensive stint as eleven-man Leeds hung on for a 6-5 win over Featherstone Rovers before showing the first signs of his versatility and dependability when picked as full-back to face Wigan the following afternoon, also at a rain-sodden Headingley. Although he was just unable to prevent Trevor Lake making it 3-3 at the break with a flying dive in at the corner, he twice produced memorable tackles to prevent Lake again and then Dave Bolton as the Loiners produced a storming finish to win 16-3. Two days later he added to his growing 'play anywhere' reputation by appearing at centre in the return match against Featherstone, just being denied in a late long-range raid which might have yielded a draw.

He received more rave reviews after Leeds grafted out a midweek win at home to Hull, a match notorious for winger Eddie Ratcliffe deliberately heading the ball forward from a wayward pass before re-gathering while the shocked Airlie Birds stood around in disbelief. Although Ratcliffe was tackled, from the resulting play-the-ball, Mick quickly darted clear to send debutant Australian trialist centre Dennis Burke over for the crucial score in a 21-16 success. A try, when he showed neat invention to kick through for himself on the wing in defeat at Warrington, was followed by an inspired Man of the Match performance as Workington were downed in Leeds' eleventh home win on the trot. With the scores level at the break Shoey – having already fashioned a touchdown for Don Robinson with a typical supporting burst – exploded into life to dominate the proceedings. He swooped on a loose ball from a scrum 30 yards out and hacked on to score before creating a try for linking full-back George Simpson and grabbed his first brace for the club when pouncing on another loose ball to canter round to the posts. Again the newspapers extolled Mick's contributions, the *Green Final* running a feature centred on him whilst looking at the future for the club. 'The big talking point among Leeds supporters arising from recent matches has been the development of scrum-half Michael Shoebottom', it began. 'Shoebottom was the best Leeds player at Warrington last Monday and outstanding against Workington last Wednesday. Indeed his display against Workington was as good as anything produced by any Leeds player all season and it would appear that, in this well-built and very keen youngster, the Headingley club have got a first-class prospect. The big hope is that from the crop of youngsters Leeds have signed in recent times; others of the same calibre of Shoebottom will emerge. A vast amount of junior Rugby League recruiting has been done by Leeds because it is becoming increasingly difficult to sign established stars and big names from Rugby Union.' His final two appearances of a campaign which fizzled out owing to the fixture backlog both ended in injury, a calf strain reducing his mobility, if not his enthusiasm, in a win at home over Hull Kingston Rovers, while he left the field on a stretcher in a defeat after a typically robust clash at Castleford.

Team-mate Ray Batten remembers those early days with obvious affection. 'The first time I met Michael, he was playing 'A' team football. I think he had been at Headingley for about a year when I signed and together with Barry Seabourne we formed a midfield triangle and more or less grew up together in that environment. He was so exuberant and very fit and had the ability to play in any position – you just had to find somewhere to put him because he was such a tremendous player. He was a character, always laughing and joking, tremendously hard on the field but a gentleman off it, a really nice guy.'

During the summer Mick was one of a number of the code's most promising youngsters invited to spend a week of intensive training at Bisham Abbey under the guidance of Rugby League staff coaches Albert Fearnley, Laurie Gant and Colin Hutton. It was also here that he came under the tutelage of former Leeds great Bert Cook, who broke a host of goal-kicking records after arriving from New Zealand in 1947 along with Arthur Clues. His manner and approach in getting the message across to the eager emerging players left a lasting impression, as Mick later acknowledged. Accompanying him on the camp was current Leeds Rhinos chief scout and Academy team manager Bob Pickles, who also hailed from Hunslet and enjoyed many distinguished years as a half-back at Parkside. 'Mick came down with back-rower Dave Walker from Headingley and we played and trained together as the elite Under-20s of the day. I was the youngest but it was a fantastic time where we all got to know each other really well. I'd already come across Mick from playing for Hunslet Schools even though I was a couple of years below him, and whenever we got together we always had good fun and a great time together.'

'On the Wednesday afternoon they gave us time off and some of the lads got the train to London but a group of us, including Dougie Laughton, Colin Clarke, Paul Daley and Colin Whitfield, jumped onto the buses for Marlow. It was just at the height of Beatlemania and as soon as we hit the town and the girls heard our northern accents they loved us because they thought we must have lived next door to them. Mick and I met these two very good-looking young ladies who had a mini, which was something really special at the time and they arranged to meet us again on the Friday night and said they'd call for us. Bisham Abbey was an old monastery and once you threw the big old wooden doors open there was this long corridor down to the dining room which had its own doors wedged open because it was a typically warm evening. We were sitting in there finishing our meals and being spoken to by the coaching team when you could hear this clip-clopping coming from the entrance and suddenly the girls were there saying to us, "we've come for you boys, are you out now?". Everyone in the room was absolutely amazed and we took some stick off them but we had a great night.'

'There was a fair on all the time we were there because it was a week before the Henley Regatta and a lot of events were taking place on the river, but when it came to the end of the evening on that Wednesday at about half ten, eleven o'clock, we didn't know how to get home or where we were going. Terry Fogerty started chatting up this bloke in the pub we were in who owned a baker's van saying, "come on, give us a lift back and we'll all give you so much apiece." He wouldn't have it at first but Terry kept on nattering to him until eventually he gave in and he said all right, "but you don't take anything out of the back". Terry got us all together and gave us this serious speech like, "you've heard him lads, we're very grateful to this gentleman and nobody touches a thing". About a dozen of us all climbed in this van and when we got back we all piled into one of the rooms and someone said, "right, what've you got?" and we all opened our coats and there were cream cakes, scones, tea cakes, éclairs and we just had a brilliant midnight feast.'

Mick shows his prowess on attack and defence during a week of elite training at the Centre Council for Physical Recreation's facility at Bisham Abbey (14-21 June 1963).

Some of the happy band gathered at Bisham Abbey pose for a group portrait, including back row: Albert Fearnley, George Shepherd, Terry Fogerty, Keith Pollard, Colin Hutton. Middle row: Bert Cook, Cliff Wallis, Alan Newbound, Doug Laughton, Tony Barrow, Colin Clarke, Ray Abbey, Laurie Gant. Front row: Derek Whitehead, Tony Karalius, Mick Shoebottom, Chris Young, Bob Pickles, Paul Daley.

'On the training pitch Mick was his usual competitive self. We were split into four teams and we were doing this high jump exercise and I went first and decided to do this forward dive over the bar but came off worse when I wrenched my back. Mick saw me but thought "that's for me" and just bombed over in exactly the same manner.' Doug Laughton, then beginning a star-studded career at St Helens, remembers the high jump incident with particular chagrin. 'We were doing a lot of drill sessions like side stepping and sprinting and Mick was ahead in most of them. When it came to the high jump I was winning but the next thing he just came in and dived over the bar head first – and this was years before Fosbury. I said "you can't do that" because I was very upset at losing my lead, and I certainly wasn't going to do it like that, but the coaching staff allowed it. That just showed his crazy side but he hated losing, he was such a tough competitor. He played the game as I think it should be played and never went out there with any other thought than to win.'

The growing calls for his regular inclusion in the Loiners ranks began with the opening fixture of the 1963/64 season, when his sparkling performance ensured Leeds just won their traditional Lazenby Cup curtain raiser against Hunslet, then newly promoted from the second division. Recurrent ankle injuries, a legacy of his earlier dislocation, then hampered his availability anyway but as the men from Headingley started the season in poor fashion under coach Trevor Foster – winning only three of their first eleven games in the league – the fans' impatience increased. A number of them vented their concern in the letters column of the local newspapers. 'D.T.' of Leeds 15 summed up the mood when writing, 'Good team man and hard worker though he is, Evans is not of the same calibre as Shoebottom and his replacement by that player would soon bring more results from Rees and Co.' Mick returned to top line action in early December, scoring a try in defeat at Widnes and performing heroically in defence at centre for a surprise, narrow home win over a Castleford side that had been unbeaten in eight previous matches. Inconsistency may have dogged the side but Mick's obvious enthusiasm at last began to spark their attack as 1964 began. He scored two tries from scrum-half with outrageous dummies as Hull Kingston Rovers were beaten at

Mick is powerless to prevent Dave Sampson crossing for Wakefield in a Championship clash at Belle Vue on 28 December 1963, Trinity completing an easy double in the space of three days.

Headingley, the £8,000 signing from Hull, Dick Gemmell, breaking a leg in that game twenty minutes into his debut, and seemed to relish a fleeting partnership with Lewis Jones who was moved back to stand-off in his final few matches before emigrating to Australia.

The somewhat surprise sale of Colin Evans to York on the eve of the Challenge Cup seemed to herald Mick's elevation up the pecking order although Leeds were defeated in the first round of the competition at Salford without scoring a point. An outstanding 14-6 win at St Helens in February, Leeds' first at Knowsley Road for seventeen seasons, was the remaining highlight of a disappointing campaign. He fashioned an early score for Brian Shaw with a lovely reverse pass and was the key ground maker as Drew Broatch crossed to establish an 8-point lead in as many minutes. Ray French, who was in the opposing ranks, was one who quickly spotted Mick's value. 'I first came across him when I was at Saints and he was a youngster. They were always big games against Leeds but he was a tough lad even then. He had this very upright stance when he ran with the ball and could lay it off beautifully. He also had a very high step which made him a difficult bloke to tackle head on because his knees and legs would come up at you everywhere and he had a superb side step. He had good timing and judgment but he was hard and he loved the physical commitment.'

The secret behind that surprise success over the border appeared to lie in recently appointed coach Roy Francis' decision to allow and encourage his players to attend the 'Rugby League Queen's' dance at Headingley the night before, young centre Robin Dewhurst and Mick with their respective partners taking first and second in the Twist competition. Francis, who enjoyed an illustrious playing career and had begun to make a name for himself as a coach at Hull where he had reached nine finals, was tempted to Headingley to restore the fortunes of the dormant giant. His arrival and influence was germane to the hastened development of young talent in the club, as Ken Eyre notes. 'Just as Mick was breaking through, Lewis Jones was leaving for Australia and a lot of the Leeds crowd thought it was the end of an era. I prefer to think they had no need to worry. Lewis was rightly revered, I only had the privilege of playing with him once for a combined Leeds side against New Zealand under lights at Headingley in the early '60s and he was marvellous, outstanding, you could just tell. But in my book the influence he brought to the side from the mid-'50s was on a par with what Shoey did in his time although they did it in different ways; I can give Mick no greater accolade. I was having a conversation with Roy Francis one day when I was out with one of my numerous broken arms and I asked him about some of his early signings at Headingley that I used to read about when I was at Hunslet, the likes of Bill Drake, Alan Lockwood and Les Chamberlain, all experienced guys. He told me it was because he had to buy some time, he was more excited about the potential he could see in the second team but he couldn't bring it through all at once. He said that the biggest factor in the end was Lewis' decision to finish. There was no way Roy or the club would have retired him, it wouldn't have been deserved, but while Lewis was there those coming through like Shoey were waiting for him to call the play and maybe not doing what they were good at. These young lads were stymied; Mick couldn't do what Roy wanted him to or what he was capable of even at that early age. When Lewis left Roy was able to put him at stand-off, which is where he'd earmarked him, because of the way he ran at people.' Alan Smith could sense the wind of change that was running through the club. 'When I arrived Shoey was already there with Robin Dewhurst and Trevor Oldroyd as one of the up-and-coming youngsters but he featured in the first team then before any of us and I know that when Roy Francis arrived in '63 he immediately spotted Mick's potential. The team from '62/63 changed dramatically and, although timing is everything, in Roy Francis we had somebody who could bring the youth policy together and make it work.'

A highly significant half-back selection for the Lazenby Cup clash to open the 1964/65 proceedings saw teenagers Mick Shoebottom and Barry Seabourne in harness at the start of what was to become a sizzling, hugely productive partnership over the next six seasons. Reviving their early exploits from schooldays, enjoyment was clearly the key behind their later success, as Barry points out. 'In those early days he was the skinniest kid I had ever seen, before he arrived at Leeds, he was like a flea. As he grew and filled out, he got the power to go with his enthusiasm. He was all aggression combined with tremendous pace and he would be the tops in the modern game, he would have made a fantastic loose forward especially with ten metres to play in. His speed was also in his ability to read the game and be in the right place just like Ellery Hanley, if you made a half break you knew he would be round there somewhere. He was always so happy, no matter what he was always laughing. The John Smith's advertisement where they are practicing their football skills sums him up perfectly – Shoey would have been the one who blasted the ball out of the ground. A lot of times at training we would have the odd game of football and if Mick was faced with an open goal you could almost guarantee he would smash it over the bar. We were all living the dream playing up at Leeds. Work during the week was the means to an end, we were just desperate to get up to the ground and train and be together. Mick was always a leading light socially, if anything was going on after training he would be there. We used to play snooker at the Bowling Club or go to the Star and Garter in Kirkstall, and in the summer Mick loved his cricket. He was a Freddie Trueman type, he liked to try and hurt the opposition or the ball!'

Mick scored both of the Loiners' tries in a comfortable 18-2 win at Parkside that afternoon, and, but for a forward pass, he would have had a second half hat-trick. Although a 'friendly' fixture, if such a term could be applied to a passionate local derby where both sides characteristically contained a number who had graced the other's ranks, it said much about desire and willingness ahead of the forthcoming fray. Always eager to impress, Mick's record in the fixture spoke volumes for his determination and competitiveness. In each of the five subsequent Lazenby ties he played in against his 'home' club he never failed to score, amassing eight tries, four goals and a drop goal in the process. By then Bob Pickles was a doughty opponent. 'I first came up against him professionally in the Lazenby Cup and he was a great player; a fine, strong lad who'd do you a job in any position. In the modern game today, with all the swapping and changing around of players within matches, Mick Shoebottom would be the perfect man to have around. You wouldn't fear any of your players on the field getting injured because Mick could cover for all of them. He was such an exciting talent at everything and he never wanted to lose at anything. Even though I was with Hunslet, we knew or grew-up with most of the Leeds lads, and especially after the week away at Bisham with Mick, there was a real camaraderie amongst all the players in the city. Whenever the sides were playing away we used to meet in town at the Lyons Tea Rooms before catching the coach and then afterwards meet up at the Ridings Hotel or The Whip. The minute you walked through the door in either of those places, your pint was waiting on the bar for you.'

The Loiners' squad that set out on the 1964 Yorkshire Cup trail, eventually reaching the final against Wakefield at Huddersfield. From left to right, back row: Joyce, Neumann, Towler, Davies, Drake, Shoebottom, Thomas, Wrigglesworth. Front row: Seabourne, Chamberlain, Gemmell, Smith, Oldroyd, Dewhurst.

This was a season of steady improvement and consolidation for Francis' men, his youngsters in particular gaining invaluable experience and reaching their first final for three seasons. That came in the Yorkshire Cup, with Hunslet and Keighley easily beaten at Headingley in September, Shoey warming up for the semi-final at Halifax's Thrum Hall with another spellbinding hat-trick as Batley were easily beaten at Mount Pleasant in the Championship. His form was good enough to merit his first inclusion in a representative squad as he was named among the reserves for Yorkshire in both of their impending County Championship clashes against Cumberland at Whitehaven and Lancashire in Hull. A back injury looked as though it might scupper his chances of playing in the semi but intensive treatment paid off as he produced his finest performance in the blue and amber to date. The game was precariously balanced, Leeds 9-7 ahead following a fine long-range try from Ronnie Cowan in the first half. From then on they were forced into desperate, scrambling defence as the home forwards continually battered their line before Mick nipped in for two dazzling tries in eight minutes around the hour mark to clinch a glorious win on a notoriously difficult ground. The first illustrated his uncanny ability to support at just the right time, beautifully sidestepping Robinson and James after hooker Alan Lockwood, Dick Gemmell and Ernest Towler had split the 'Fax ranks while his second was a stunning diagonal burst to the corner from half way after another fine reverse pass from Gemmell. The impending final at Huddersfield's Fartown ground had added poignancy being against Wakefield, the side he could so easily have been playing for. 'I've never regretted going to Headingley', Mick told the *Daily Mail*'s Brian Batty in the lead up to the game, 'and now I'm going to show Trinity what they missed', he added. 'Mike is certainly the man Trinity fear most' Batty continued in his preview, but the match turned out to be one of his biggest disappointments despite receiving a heartwarming 'congratulations and best wishes' telegram from his old mates at Bison Bulls in the dressing room just before the kick-off. Neil Fox returned to his best form for Trinity and grabbed 12 points from two tries and three goals while former sprint champion Berwyn Jones benefited from Trinity's bewildering ability to keep the ball alive to race over for a brace of touchdowns in a comprehensive 18-2 success.

Tries in three of the next four matches including setting up a barnstorming Headingley finale to beat Leigh, and a swashbuckling Man of the Match display to subdue Dewsbury showed that the precocious youngster had quickly put the cup setback behind him, which further endeared him to the Loiners fans. His 75-yard spectacular solo effort to open the

A good luck telegram from his former team mates at Bisons.

scoring against Dewsbury brought a standing ovation from the crowd of just under 4,000 and prompted a *Green Post* editorial to comment, '...the driving force of Shoebottom becomes increasingly valuable, and, while he keeps fit and in present form, there is not much chance for Alan Rees to get back into first team action.' Unfortunately, unbeknown to the writer, there was a double irony in his analysis. Although Mick was again a key figure as Hull were taken apart at the Boulevard, including kicking his first four goals for the club and against Castleford when his fifty-fifth minute penalty secured the spoils, persistent leg problems hampered his progress. In early January 1965 he was carried off with another collapse of his suspect ankle joint – which he always assiduously strapped up before a game – at Doncaster, his hoped for recovery suffering a further setback when he was involved in a car accident on the way to training a fortnight later which saw him badly shaken. Although he returned to play in a victory over Liverpool City in the first round of the Challenge Cup, his season was virtually over after operations which saw him with his foot in plaster and enduring another frustrating lengthy absence.

Earlier in the campaign, his rich promise had seen Oldham launch a bid for Rees, the former Welsh Rugby Union international and Glamorgan cricketer, but towards the end of the season Mick was considering his own future at the club and put in a transfer request which was immediately rejected. Part of the reason was that he felt he was likely to lose his favoured stand-off berth, Scotsman Drew Broatch being touted for the position aided by his selection for the 'Other Nationalities' in the number six shirt while some pundits claimed that, despite Mick's obvious verve and elusiveness, his style of play was too individual and was not bringing the best out of the Leeds back division. Secretary of Leeds at the time, Bill Carter, confirms that Mick did think about trying his hand elsewhere. 'He did ask for a transfer but that was just his impetuousness to get into the first team. He always thought that he was good enough – without being boastful in any way, that wasn't part of his nature – but we were anxious to nurse him along in those early stages. We were only looking after his interests and gradually getting him accustomed to the physicality of the game.' Alan Hardisty, who was often to vie with him for representative jerseys and rated him second only to Alex Murphy as his most difficult opponent, revealed in his biography that their early battles at club level were part of Mick's learning curve. 'There was always a smack or two off Mick, but he told me in Australia that, "That got me many bollockings from Roy Francis at half-time." Before the game, Roy would grab hold of Mick and say "Now this Hardisty, don't leave him for a minute, stick to him, sort the bugger out." And for the first ten or twenty that's all Mick would do, just stand opposite where he thought I was behind the forwards. Then he'd think, "Well, he's not bothering today" and he'd get stuck into the game. Next thing I'm under the sticks and Roy is going spare with Mick at half-time...But that was Mick, he wanted to be involved all the time.'

Shoey need not have worried. Fully recovered during the summer off-season, Leeds signed former Wakefield scrum-half Ken Rollin and the two struck up an instant rapport on and off the field, added to which one of Mick's best friends from his Hunslet schooldays, Syd Hynes, had made quite an impression on his debut in the final match of the 1964/65

Opposite: An avid sportsman, all-rounder Mick polishes his bat in readiness for the new cricket season with 'Slazengers'.

campaign after signing from Leeds NALGO. Bill Carter saw the transformation. 'Mick used to get a bit keyed up before matches but once he was on the pitch he was never bothered. I think he just worried beforehand in case he didn't do well. He thrived when Syd arrived and improved as a player under the influence of Ken Rollin. Ken Thornett thought the world of him and his cavalier style too.'

5

BACK WITH A BANG

One defeat, away at Hull, in their first six games represented a more than satisfactory start to the 1965/66 season for the Loiners, with Mick again in the thick of the action. He produced a dominant display to help scupper Bradford Northern at Odsal and was at his cheeky best at Hunslet, as his niece Vicky Parkin recalls. 'I went to watch him at Parkside with a friend of mine. I was about eleven or twelve at the time and we were standing at the railings at one of the ends behind the posts. Mick really fooled me when he went down in a heavy-looking tackle near the line and lay prone on the ground, presumably looking for a penalty. I thought he was really hurt and couldn't help myself running on to the pitch to see how he was. He just rolled over, winked at me and whispered, "Get back behind those sticks" before playing on. Two policemen then came and stood by us and said "And don't do that again young lady", which frightened the life out of me but made Mick laugh when I told him.'

Another superb performance came against the New Zealand tourists where former Leeds hero, Australian winger Eric Harris, selected him as the Benson & Hedges Award winner for the hosts. His interception and teasing kick nearly brought a try for Ronnie Cowan and twice he was hauled down just short of glory as Leeds gallantly fought back from 14-2 down to trail by just a point, before running out of steam owing to mounting injuries in the final quarter. It was the kind of showing against top-quality opposition that began persistent calls throughout the year from various quarters for Mick to be included in the Lions tour party at the end of the campaign, despite, somewhat surprisingly, missing out on selection for Yorkshire early in the season. Soon after, though, at York, his fortunes saw him turn from hero to villain when he was sent off and subsequently banned for two matches. Trevor Watson described the incident in the *Yorkshire Evening Post*. 'Tees was sent off after a tackle on Shoebottom. Shoebottom was sent off ten minutes from time after Fowler was hurt in a tackle.' There was more trauma in the Shoebottom household when George, a lorry driver for 'Yorkshire Copper Works', suffered severe industrial injuries when metal from a forklift truck fell on him. 'I broke my neck and back in 1965 in a work accident; I can remember Mick coming all the way down to Devon to see me with some flowers because I was initially only given twelve hours to live, so I missed a number of matches while he was breaking through but I was always there home and away if I could be, and the first to tell if he'd had a bad game – which was hardly ever.'

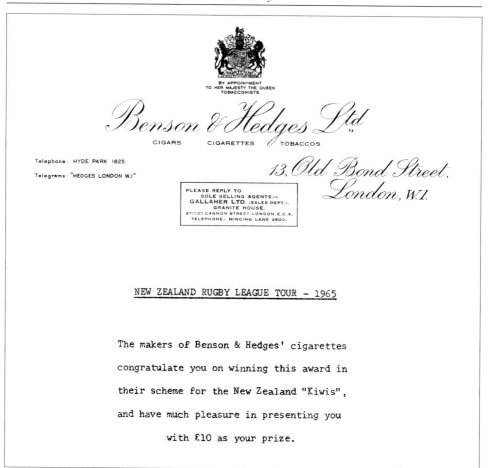

BY APPOINTMENT
TO HER MAJESTY THE QUEEN
TOBACCONISTS

Benson & Hedges Ltd.

CIGARS   CIGARETTES   TOBACCOS

Telephone: HYDE PARK 1825

Telegrams: "HEDGES LONDON W.I"

13, Old Bond Street,
London, W.I.

PLEASE REPLY TO
SOLE SELLING AGENTS :—
GALLAHER LTD. (SALES DEPT.),
GRANITE HOUSE,
97/101 CANNON STREET, LONDON. E.C.4.
TELEPHONE : MINCING LANE 2800.

NEW ZEALAND RUGBY LEAGUE TOUR - 1965

The makers of Benson & Hedges' cigarettes

congratulate you on winning this award in

their scheme for the New Zealand "Kiwis",

and have much pleasure in presenting you

with £10 as your prize.

Benson & Hedges congratulate Mick on being Leeds' Man of the Match during the Kiwis Rugby League Tour in 1965.

A relatively poor September for the side, which included elimination from the Yorkshire Cup at the hands of Huddersfield, saw the Headingley management make two key signings of experienced players who gave the perfect lead to the impressionable youngsters coming through. Mick revelled in the tutelage of revered Australian full-back Ken Thornett who was flown back for a short-term stint to solve an injury crisis while Great Britain loose forward Harry Poole was captured from Hull Kingston Rovers to drive the pack and skipper the side. Thornett's arrival was principally as cover for Robin Dewhurst – who had again succumbed to a long-standing knee injury and needed further surgery – which saw Mick briefly inherit the goal-kicking role again. Coached by his incapacitated close friend in the art, Shoey's first success came in the newly sanctioned BBC2 Floodlit Trophy competition at Castleford, his conversion and angled penalty securing a thrilling 7-7 draw for the new television audience. Five goals against Leigh, his best haul to date, was followed by a spectacular long pass to uncover Dick Gemmell for the opening try against Featherstone, Mick's 10 of 13 points – which included a trademark long-distance touchdown – finally accounting for Rovers and maintaining a rich vein of form. However, it soon became obvious that although he could be relied upon as a back-up emergency goal-kicker, it was not his forte and he missed nine consecutive shots at goal in the home drubbing of Batley. His final match as first-choice kicker coincided with Thornett's eleventh and last of his second spell in the blue and amber in early January 1966 against Castleford, and Mick paid one of his mentors his own tribute by claiming all the points in a breathtaking 8-7 victory. Thornett's parting shot was to leave a message for the Great Britain selectors, imploring them to pick Shoey and his eighteen-year-old adversary from that match Roger Millward, both of whom had by then been named in the shadow squad, for the Tests against France which doubled as tour trials. 'They are indispensable especially on the hard grounds out there. Mick showed the value of his instinctive support play with his two tries and Roger's attacking flashes nearly took the match from us', Thornett said afterwards. Respected Rugby League journalist and broadcaster Eddie Waring agreed. After Mick had fashioned a double over Bradford he wrote, 'Mick Shoebottom had a great game. Shoebottom has improved in every aspect of his game and on this form he must be considered a candidate for a tour place.'

Another selection masterstroke by Roy Francis was his choice of who to replace Thornett and cure the goal-kicking dilemma for good measure, an inspired signing bringing Bev Risman across the Pennines from Leigh. His debut was against Dewsbury at Headingley at the beginning of February and although he kicked three goals, it was Mick who stole the headlines with another superb all-action display, leading to more glowing testimonials, especially in the *Green Post*. The article began, 'Mick Shoebottom produced another power-house display and in his tackling as in his attacking bursts he showed both football skill of a high order and a never-say-die spirit that we now come to associate with almost everything he does', before continuing with '…the part played in this, and in fact all of the Leeds victory run of 1966, by off-half Mick Shoebottom, must not go unnoticed nor unrecorded. There can be few men as tireless and strong, playing in this key position today.'

It did not take long for Risman to appreciate the quality of the man he had in front of him. 'When I transferred to Leeds, one of the most pleasing thoughts was that I would now be a team-mate of Mick's rather than an opponent. He was the most amazing character in the dressing room because he was frightened of nobody and he had all these nervous expressions before the game as everyone was warming up and getting prepared. He'd just be standing there shouting things like, "let me (expletive) get at them, I can't wait, come on lads let's get out there and get stuck in".'

'Every single game was the same, it didn't matter who we were up against, whether it was Bramley or Wigan, that's how he played the game. He was everything, perpetual motion, a human dynamo, whether we had the ball or the opposition did, and the big thing about him was that he was basically thirteen defenders and if anybody missed a tackle Shoey was there to tidy it up. The energy he had was just unbelievable. Any time there was any rough stuff, he was in there. Bill Ramsey was the enforcer but Shoey was the one who finished it off no matter which member of the opposition threatened anything. He was a great attacker because he was so strong. A modern-day equivalent would be a Kevin Sinfield type, a good footballer with the ball in his hands and using his strength to break tackles. He wasn't the fanciest of players but he could step off both feet, move the ball, kick and do everything that was necessary, but the thing he loved most was getting stuck in. He found training easy because

Above left: Ken Thornett, the veteran Australian full-back, had a massive impact on Mick's early career.

Above right: A cartoon from *Speed*.

he was one of these fellows who could run all day; he smoked and drank a bit but it didn't affect him, he'd just got an engine that could go forever.'

'Being under Roy Francis was what made him. He just took on board everything Roy told him, followed it out to the letter and did more. Even arriving as a senior player, he taught me a lot. I was behind him and had the best appreciation of what he could do; I think I made about two tackles all season. One of the things he was best at was his anticipation. Sometimes he would go in and take the forwards out and other times he would just wait to see what happened and covered every break that was made. The opposition would be coming towards me and I would be wondering what was going to happen and then a body would come flying out of nowhere and it was always Shoey and every time he tackled anybody they really felt it because he came in with such pace. He wasn't a big lad but he was a naturally strong, wiry type and his timing of tackles was tremendous. Everybody thought it was just a physical thing with him but he could play football as well. He put 100 per cent into everything he did, on and off the field. He was simply great to be around and a wonderful bloke with it; nobody could say a bad word about him.'

By now Mick was becoming a recognized figure and enjoying the trappings of his increasing success, as Vicky Parkin confirms. 'All the kids in the neighbourhood we lived in looked forward to "uncle Shoey" coming round, especially after he bought a Morris Minor because very few people had a car near us. Bonfire Night was always memorable, he used to drive round and my friends would queue up to be swept off their feet and held up in the air by him. Often, when he visited, he would take me into Leeds and always held my hand when we crossed the road, standing between me and the traffic. Even as I got older he used to insist that I stood away from the roadside – it left such an impression on me that I now do it with my own kids.'

'He was an avid shopper and always wanted the best, whether it was clothes, food or jewellery. I can see him now in H. Samuel's buying a beautiful charm with a ten shilling note. In his earlier days when he lived at home, he used to drive his mum mad because he would never buy one shirt, he had to get two or three, and even in his later years when we went searching for some jeans he had to have two pairs in case one wore out.' Ken Eyre has similar memories. 'He liked clothes; he'd buy everything he saw if he could. He used to come up to training and I'd ask "have you seen that new car, that new model Ford?", and he'd reply "yeah, I've test driven it", but invariably he hadn't.'

Writing a feature at the beginning of March, three weeks before the British squad was due to be named, *Daily Sketch* reporter Alan Smith noted that relief over giving up the kicking duties had further enhanced Mick's credentials. 'Mike Shoebottom was never in any doubt over his goal-kicking pedigree,' he noted. 'He was a muggins. He took over the shots at Leeds because somebody vaguely recalled that he was a bit of a marksman in the junior game. As an enthusiast who doesn't like to refuse, he sometimes found himself teeing up the ball because other players, who might have been called on to take a chance, suddenly found a bootlace was loose…the lively stand-off is playing so well without the burden of the goal-kicks that he already has one foot on the plane taking the British Tourists to Australia this summer. One of the selectors told me: "Shoebottom is moving in with a lot of support for the tour party." A Leeds official said: "When he no longer had to kick the goals, it took a lot off Mike's mind. He is terribly keen to go to Australia." Shoebottom is now buzzing at the right time.'

Thirteen consecutive wins, resulting predominantly from outstanding defence, took Leeds into play-off contention in the Championship and through to the third round of the Cup to face Warrington at Wilderspool. Never one to need an additional incentive, Mick had good cause to perform, Wire stand-off Willie Aspinwall having gained the British Selectors' nod to the bemusement of many, including former Hunslet and Halifax star Harry Beverley, who had been a Lion in 1936. He publicly stated that Shoey's omission was a mistake which would be regretted as 'Mick would undoubtedly be a success in Australia. He would be a natural out there.' There was no doubting that he won the personal duel with Aspinwall in a war of attrition which finished 2-2, the replay forcing the Loiners to undertake a punishing schedule of six matches in eleven days over the Easter period. One of those was the traditional derby clash at Hunslet, which Harry Jepson recalls with a wry smile. 'I remember him playing at Parkside in 1966 and we'd just signed a very good lad from Cardiff called Phil Morgan at stand-off. Hunslet were playing up-hill in what was a very close game and he came off his left foot and beat Shoey on the outside – which Michael didn't like – and I remember saying to the Hunslet board, "if he can beat Shoebottom, then we've got a class player".'

Four consecutive defeats put paid to any lingering title hopes although Mick was valiant in defeat at Wakefield in a very young side which saw him link up well with Syd Hynes, but that failed to dampen the enthusiasm of a 14,000 crowd, three times the usual average, for the re-match with Warrington. A severe rib injury early on curtailed Mick's involvement, Hynes coming on as a replacement for him as Ronnie Cowan's brace of touchdowns saw Leeds home 8-0. The bruising was so acute that Mick was forced out of the semi-final at Huddersfield against Wigan; Billy Boston's only try of an excruciating, nerve-wracking game sending the Riversiders to Wembley. It must have been serious to keep him out because, as Leeds staff man Billy Watts notes, Mick was one of the bravest players he has come across. 'Injuries never seemed to bother him. I remember one time he got a very bad gash on his knee and he was stitched, leaving the two bits stuck up at the ends. Bill Carter's office in those days was a little wooden affair near the entrance gates and on Saturday afternoons I used to call in to help Bill and John Wilson out with the money from the pools. Mick came in and asked, "Have you got a pair of scissors?" We said we had and asked him why he wanted them, and then he rolled his trousers up and showed us his wound claiming the bits of metal were digging into him. He got the scissors and pulled all the stitches out, looked down and just said, "it'll heal" and walked away. That was Mick, if he got a knock he never moaned and if you wanted to play it hard he could play it hard. Equally he was just as good a footballer.'

Ever the pragmatist, he quickly put the end of season disappointments behind him with a terrific start to the 1966/67 campaign as Roy Francis' patient team-building and tactical astuteness began to pay off. Those close to him acknowledge that Shoey was buoyed by a vote of confidence expressed by Football Chairman Jack Myerscough. Writing in the Supporter's Club Handbook he said, 'Mick Shoebottom must surely be destined for international honours. As he matures he is increasing in more than physical stature, and his lionhearted displays evoke our admiration.' It was an epithet that became synonymous with him. By now John Atkinson was aware that Mick's presence was a vital ingredient in what was to follow. 'I didn't really get to know him until I broke into the first team, and [with Mick] it was like somebody had a light switch and when rugby was involved it was turned on and his whole personality changed. Off the field he was out and about but the minute he walked into the dressing room, whether it was for a match or training, he would shine, he just lived for the game. He'd start getting changed straightaway and all he wanted to do was just get out there on the field. Never, in all the years I was with him, did I see him down or depressed about anything to do with rugby, he just loved it. Results may even have come second to his total and utter commitment to the game, it was his life. You'd be getting ready for training and it might be throwing it down outside and you might not fancy it but Mick'd be round picking you up saying, "come on, let's get it done, couple of hours that's all and it'll be over, let's go", the whole dressing room was alive with him.'

A dramatic dive to post a try at Hunslet's Parkside ground in the 1966 season-opening Lazenby Cup clash.

A typically spectacular solo effort in the Lazenby Cup clash with Hunslet followed by another livewire display to down Bramley as they opened their new £30,000 McLaren Field complex, put down an early marker, but it was Mick's performance at home to Keighley that finally opened the Yorkshire selectors' eyes. Arthur Haddock in the *Yorkshire Evening Post* extolled, 'Although Leeds beat Keighley 17-5 at Headingley there was only one real difference in performance between the sides. This came from Leeds off-half Shoebottom, who gave a terrific display and made the win a "one-man-band" affair. His skill and dash brought him two brilliant tries...Shoebottom's zip stood out like a beacon.' The *Yorkshire Post*'s correspondent Alfred Drewry was equally effusive. 'He stood out above all the others for ingenuity, quickness, industry and the aptitude for doing the right thing at the right time which lifts a player out of the ordinary rut.' That was a prelude to an even more devastating performance on the afternoon the County committee sat down to pick the side against Cumberland when he tore hapless Batley apart at Mount Pleasant. Four tries and nine goals saw him end 1 point short of Lewis Jones' tally in a match record for the club and become the first player for nine years to score 30 points in a game on a day when the Loiners honoured the passing of one of their finest players, representatives and ambassadors 'Dinny' Campbell, who had died in his native Australia. Club secretary Bill Carter witnessed the feat, 'Mick wasn't aware how close he came to breaking the club points record at Batley nor was he disappointed when he found out that he was one short of it, especially when he realized that he would have been taking it from Lewis Jones. He hero-worshipped Lewis and, having made his debut with him, rated him very, very highly. I chatted to Mick just afterwards about it and I think he felt that he would have been unworthy of taking the place of someone he kept saying was such a fantastic player.' Leeds winger Alan Smith subsequently heard how it

Shoey scorches for the line and leaves the Castleford defence trailing in a 23-2 success at Headingley on 26 August 1966.

No stopping the blonde blur as he finds a gap in the Wigan defence at Headingley on 17 September 1966. *(Picture by Irvine Crawford)*

felt for the stricken Gallant Youths. 'Brian Harrison, who is now my partner in business, played for Batley that day and he tells the tale of how he was a Yorkshire schoolboy and at Mount Pleasant he was viewed as an outstanding junior especially being a local lad but once he came up against Leeds that day it was a real lesson. He can remember Shoey stampeding through and somehow Brian was the last man but he couldn't get within 5 yards of Mick, he just flew round him.'

The expansive style of the Francis ideal was evidently tailor-made for Mick's boundless energy, and the pre-season regime the coach had put his charges through to increase fitness levels was clearly paying off as Leeds posted the majority of their points in cavalier fashion late in games. It certainly seemed that the Loiners had adapted themselves to the new 5 yards at the play-the-ball, four tackle and double penalty rules – which had been devised to make the code a more open and entertaining spectacle – better and quicker than most other sides. They quickly headed the league table; a position they were to retain until the end of the season. As Francis noted, 'These rules are taking the game back fifteen years – and a good thing too! This is the sort of football the fans want.' Initially, though, Mick was not one who went along with the changes, feeling that they were too radical. Barry Seabourne, however, was in no doubt that Roy's methods were ahead of the time. 'The key behind Roy's success was that he got everyone working for each other. We used to have a players' bar at Headingley where the opposition would come for a drink after a game but we would kick them out after an hour or so. Our families used to join us there and once a month Roy would send Arthur Craddock out to get thirty lots of fish and chips and we would all stay together. Roy reckoned that he was a relative of Shirley Bassey as there was always singing going on. The spirit was fantastic and that was down to so many of us being local lads – although it's fair to say not many were from north of the city and there was a massive rivalry between Leeds and Hunslet in those days. There was a great balance, he brought in a few choice experienced, older players to do a job and guide the side while the youngsters came through together learning each other's style of play and strengths and weaknesses in the second team. Roy made sure that we were really fit, his basic instruction once we had made a break wherever we were on the field was just to run like hell.'

Seabourne's sentiments are echoed by Alan Smith. 'Roy had this ability to pick the right type of experienced players out to bring the youngsters along, like Kenny Rollin, Alan Lockwood, Harry Poole – he was a great leader and a great influence on Mick, looking out for him around the scrum – Bev Risman and Mick Clark. Roy would pull these guys in and they provided the link and bought the time for the new breed to come through and the team to emerge. Mick was the life and soul in the dressing room, he was robust and active, he wouldn't just get in the bath, he'd dive into it and throw the soap. He was energetic, fun and such a powerfully-built fellow. His presence was felt even as an eighteen year old and he was just the perfect pivot to base things around. Roy put us through some very rigorous training routines and the longevity of a number of our careers was because he pushed the barriers of our resistance back so that we became very, very strong and fit. Players nowadays are better conditioned and have a fantastic recovery rate but I don't know of any one of them that would be faster today from a standing start over a hundred metres than Mick.'

Another to witness Mick bloom first-hand was Ken Eyre. 'At that time, the game was changing with the advent of limited tackles, and what Roy did – and Shoey was an integral

RUGBY FOOTBALL LEAGUE

CHARITY MATCH

IN AID OF THE

ST. JOHN AMBULANCE BRIGADE

1966 TOURISTS v. REST OF LEAGUE

at
Headingley
Leeds

**SUNDAY,
6th NOVEMBER**
1966
Kick-off 3.0 p.m.

OFFICIAL PROGRAMME - 3/-
HOLDERS OF THIS PROGRAMME ARE ADMITTED FREE TO THE GROUND

Left: Mick gets a step closer to international recognition with his inclusion in the 'Rest of the League' side.

Opposite page:

Left: Match programme cover, Cumberland *v.* Yorkshire – Mick finally makes his White Rose bow.

Right: Match programme cover, Yorkshire *v.* Lancashire – a home county debut on his favourite patch.

part of it – was to get as many guys out there who could run and pass. It didn't matter where you were on the field, he stressed that the easiest way to beat a man was to run at him and pass the ball. Roy had this ability to spot and turn potential into exceptional footballers who are now classed as greats. He had the foresight and knowledge. Shoey had the guile and the power – despite doing a physical job all day and only training two nights a week. You can't imagine what he would have been like now as a full-time professional. I've seen many people run away from him, he used to petrify Austin Rhodes at St Helens; it was unbelievable. His kicking was superb, he could do anything and when he went on one of those famous arcing runs he was like a prancing horse. You could see where he was going but we just held back and admired because we couldn't get there fast enough to back him up anyway. Many's the time the forwards have looked at each other and just said, "Here he goes, he's gone". He'd cleave through the tacklers and then he'd be up on his toes and away, he was a fine sight to watch from that close up in full flight. My abiding memory of Mick coming off the field is of him always being the first into the bath. We'd be sat there gasping for breath, having a cup of tea or a beer and he'd already be singing in the water.'

An accumulation of 47 points in the opening five matches of the campaign saw Mick included as one of four new caps in the White Rose side to travel to Workington to face Cumberland, the other debutants being Bradford prop Peter Goddard, Keighley back-rower Terry Ramshaw and, most surprisingly, Leeds-born Doncaster right-winger Peter Goodchild. It was an honour that touched him deeply, as his brother George recalls. 'He was a very proud Yorkshireman and he loved it when he was selected to play for the county. He got a lot of his inspiration, right back to the Boys Club days, from the local lads.' Mick was joined in the side by club mate Geoff Wrigglesworth, who had just returned from the 1966 Tour, and Mick did enough with a crucial try just before half-time in a typically busy and highly-effective performance in a 17-17 draw to retain his place for the Roses clash at his beloved Headingley a fortnight later. A crowd of just over 10,500 were present to witness the official switching on of the new floodlights at the famous stadium, which was hosting a County Championship game for the first time in nearly twenty years, with Leeds and Great Britain skipper Harry Poole coming back to lead the Tykes. Lancashire took the glory with a thrilling 22-17 success but Mick remembered little of the encounter, suffering delayed concussion which forced him to spend two nights under observation in hospital. His inclusion for the 'Rest of the League' in early November in the first ever domestic Sunday fixture in aid of St John's Ambulance against the Great Britain Tourists at Headingley showed that he was making a significant impression on the International Selectors, but an even bigger match was looming.

Controversy looked set to reign regarding the floodlit fixture with Oldham at the Watersheddings scheduled for the night of Friday 25 November 1966, with particular

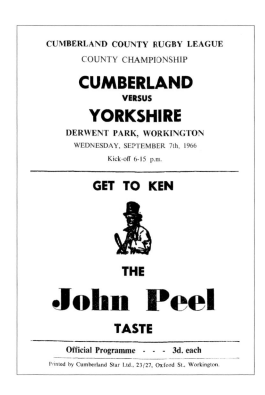

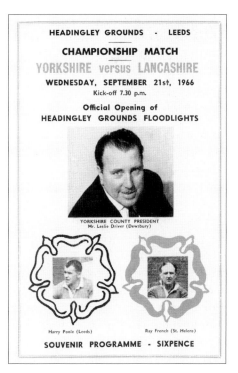

consternation in the Shoebottom household. At the last minute the hosts requested a switch to the following day, which was ironic since Leeds had initially opposed the Friday date but were forced to accede after the Rugby League Management committee agreed to it so as to avoid a clash with the Oldham Athletic *v.* Notts County FA Cup first round tie. Although Leeds pointed out the inconvenience their fans would suffer – having already rearranged their initial coach bookings and being keen for an extra day's rest before travelling to Swinton early the following week for a floodlit Trophy clash – the main reason they refused to budge again was because their star stand-off was scheduled to get married that day, with Ken Rollin as his best man and the bulk of the team on hand to proffer their congratulations. But no traditional stag night for Mick; he characteristically made himself available to play and produced his usual Trojan tackling stint, but the Loiners were narrowly defeated for only the second time that season, their only other reverse also having come in Lancashire at St Helens. Fifteen hours later, resplendent in best suit and white carnation buttonhole, he was on the steps of

No respecter of size or reputation, a typical Shoey tackle.

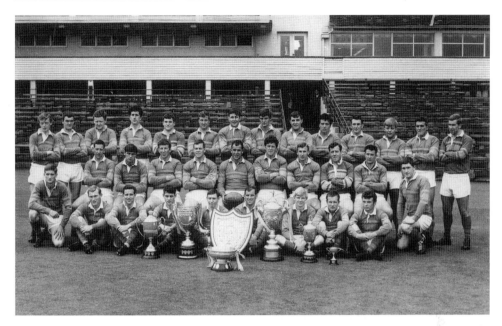

Leeds club squad 1966/67 with a hoard of the code's trophies. From left to right, back row: Robert Smith, A. Smith, Burke, Coulthard, Fozzard, A. Eyre, Sykes, Hick, Barnard, K. Eyre, Batten, Sunderland, Crosby, Brown. Middle row: Broatch, Atkinson, Clark, Gemmell, Poole, Chamberlain, Cowan, Lockwood, Hynes. Front row: Fawdington, Roger Smith, Rollin, Watson, Seabourne, Risman, Shoebottom, Astbury, Doyle, Higginbottom.

Wakefield Cathedral wreathed in smiles. Almost inevitably, it was rugby that brought him and twenty-year-old orthopaedic nurse Carol Baum together; the pair met when she treated him for his ankle problems at Pinderfields Hospital a couple of years earlier. A keen member of the Wakefield Amateur Operatic Society, Carol had little interest in the code but almost a year later their acquaintance was rekindled when Mick frequently went back to the ward to visit George, and their romance blossomed. Naturally the wedding photographs featured a rugby ball, Leeds skipper Harry Poole on hand to throw Carol a pass for the cameras before the party headed for the Three Houses Hotel at Sandal for the reception.

Leeds entered the traditionally hectic festive programme in sparkling form, young wingers Alan Smith and John Atkinson to the fore, Mick dropping his first goal for the club in a 9-6 Headingley success over Hull Kingston Rovers on Christmas Eve and scoring a try as Wakefield were humbled in front of a big Boxing Day crowd to put the Loiners 4 points clear at the top of the table. A stirring backs-to-the-wall display ended the year with a rare victory at Hull, Mick playing a crucial role on defence and leading the breakout charges in a thrilling 9-8 success, but there were worrying scenes afterwards when he and former Hull man Dick Gemmell were hurt in a flare up, the club deciding not to take the matter further. Three more convincing home wins in January virtually assured the club the Yorkshire League title, their first for six seasons, but serious injuries meant that Mick missed much of the vital run in to the Championship and another Challenge Cup saga that was cruelly, and surprisingly, ended by Featherstone at the semi-final stage. A knee problem kept him out of big league games at Castleford and Wigan before he returned to gain a measure of revenge over Oldham in Leeds'

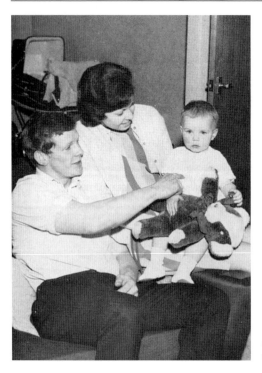

Mick relaxing at home with wife Carol and two-year-old daughter Amanda Jayne.

first cup success in Lancashire for virtually two decades. Feted in mid–March as part of the side to collect the recently instituted League Leaders' Trophy, a degenerative and worrying back problem which required hospitalization ruled him out of a quarter-final home tie with Swinton and beyond. Finishing top of the League was a major milestone for Roy Francis' fledgling outfit, as Barry Seabourne testifies. 'That was a tremendous achievement because every side we faced seemed to have three or four current or ex-internationals in their ranks. That level of competition seemed to spur us on and, as youngsters without real fear anyway, continually made us push ourselves further. Roy had by then installed this tremendous sense of belief in what we were doing and how good we were. He kept setting us targets as individuals to play for the county and then the country. Mick had two sides to his game, when we had the ball his job was to not get tackled around the scrum and provide the quick service we needed to launch the likes of John Atkinson, Alan Smith, Syd Hynes and Bernard Watson. Possession and speed was vital, especially under the four tackle rule. On defence he just looked after everybody; he loved the aggressive side of the game.'

Throughout early 1967 Mick was troubled by persistent and worsening spinal pain, the cause of which was proving to be a mystery although Leeds officials were convinced that it was caused by his frequent heavy lifting at Bison's building yard where he worked as a foreman labourer. The only way to stabilize the condition was to encase him in plaster, a drastic treatment which thankfully prevented a longer lay off at a later date. The careful recovery and gradual return to training gave him time to supervise the building of the new family home on a plot of land on the outskirts of Wakefield alongside neighbour Ken Rollin, before the advent of fatherhood with the arrival of daughter Amanda Jayne in June 1967.

6

1967/68
WATERSPLASH, WEMBLEY
AND WORLD CUP

For once the headlines were right when they screamed 'Leeds give warning' after an emphatic 34-17 pre-season Lazenby Cup success over Hunslet at Headingley. The Loiners had come so close to capturing the big prizes in the previous two seasons but 1967/68 saw the beginning of an unprecedented run of success as the promise and potential of Roy Francis' men, newly-skippered by prop Mick Clark, was finally turned into glory and silverware. Shoey announced his return to full fitness in that clash in some style, racing in for a magnificent hat-trick of tries that had his legions of fans purring and causing Alfred Drewry to comment, 'Shoebottom, returning after an injury which kept him inactive for the second half of last season, played as though he meant to make up for every minute lost.' Linking effectively in the first half with Ken Rollin, he spent the second in partnership with Barry Seabourne – a portent of what was to follow, while it was equally significant that all the Loiners' touchdowns came from their explosive back division.

John Atkinson noticed signs that hinted something special was beginning to evolve. 'Roy had set his stall out to build a side, he knew what he wanted and by late '67 into '68 he achieved it. He recognized the need for fitness but he never told the players how to play rugby. He picked you on your ability to play the game, and you stood or fell by how you performed, but he wouldn't have thought of giving us a game plan to work to. His work on fitness had started at the back end of his own playing career. He was the first person to come in and say that he didn't need to teach players how to play rugby if they'd been signed by Leeds, he just needed to get them as fit as he possibly could so that they would be able to play the kind of rugby they were capable of producing, and that's what he did really. Our only instructions were to play when the opportunity arose and react to situations as they came up. If an opponent was running through a particular hole, then we knew we had to adjust to close it. Roy was the first person to adapt to the new four tackle rule and if it had been six from the off, we would have been the ultimate considering the damage we did. He said we had to be fit to do everything within four tackles but there was no set structure. We'd got the players, like Mick, who just wanted to run all day. Training at Leeds was second to none at that particular time – he also encouraged us to do an awful lot on our own, and for the likes of Mick that was like manna from heaven.'

An advertisement in the *Green Post*.

Five tries in as many matches told only part of the story as Shoey again underlined his versatility value. He took the plaudits at stand-off as he held Featherstone at bay, conceded a penalty try for obstruction on young Huddersfield centre Paul Longstaff – earning a rebuke from referee Mr Wilson before scorching away for a 50-yard touchdown of his own – when reverting to scrum-half before filling in at centre and having a major hand in defeating Hunslet in the second round of the Yorkshire Cup. Hull taught Leeds a lesson in the semi-final of that competition but a week later the Loiners ended Bradford's 100 per cent start to the Championship at Odsal, although Shoey uncharacteristically passed up two scoring chances, knocking on with the line open on both occasions after first John Langley and then John Atkinson had done the spadework.

If the Headingley outfit had a perceived weakness, it was in the physical strength of their pack. Lightweight by comparison to some but incredibly mobile – Ray Batten now established at loose forward following Harry Poole's severe knee injury and forming a varied and inspirational midfield triangle with his 'double S' half-backs – there were concerns amongst the management that when the conditions got muddier and tougher, the Leeds forwards might be found wanting. Chairman Jack Myerscough and coach Francis were linked with numerous players, specifically Halifax's international back rower Terry Ramshaw and then put in a big offer for Hull Kingston Rovers pair Frank Foster and Bill Holliday. It was heavily rumoured that the Robins wanted Mick as part of the deal to play alongside Roger Millward and when Hunslet heard the speculation they made a seemingly facetious enquiry for his services, only to be given short shrift by Myerscough who publicly stated that his prize asset was 'not for buying'. While confirming that the club had made a £14,000 plus player bid for the duo he was at pains to stress that the offer had been turned down flat by Rovers' chairman Wilf Spaven before a Leeds player could be named, and that 'In any case we are in the market as buyers, not sellers', adding, 'We certainly cannot afford to lose a player of Shoebottom's calibre.' Hunslet's willingness to see him back on home turf is confirmed by Harry Jepson. 'Leeds wouldn't have let Michael go but it's true that we did go in for him at the time. We heard about Hull Kingston Rovers' supposed interest and we made an enquiry but Jack Myerscough wouldn't have anything to do with it.'

Such a public backing was richly rewarded as Leeds – and Shoey in particular – hit a magnificent vein of form as the year came to an end. Hunslet, Doncaster and York were swept away in a torrent of tries before the Loiners ground out two terrific victories on Humberside in the space of a fortnight. Mick's bottling up of Millward in the first clash brought rave reviews but his display to gain revenge over Hull for the Yorkshire Cup trouncing and spoil their first full game staged under floodlights at the Boulevard is remembered by many as one of his finest performances. In a side stripped of first choice backs Bev Risman, Dick Gemmell, Syd Hynes and Robin Dewhurst, and with Batten forced off at the break, Mick in concert with Barry Seabourne ruled the roost powering back Chris Davidson's kicks with punishing regularity, one such burst taking him 30 yards to the try-line without a hand being laid on him to give the visitors a 14-2 interval lead. Seabourne's unerring accuracy with the boot both for touch and goal saw him land seven successful shots, including two snap-drop goals in as many minutes, as the blue and amber reigned supreme on one of their bogey grounds. Derek Marshall wrote in his match report, 'The Leeds stand-off has rarely played better. He completely overshadowed Devonshire, and the back-flip that put Watson over for the second of his three tries was one of the finest touches of the match.' George Shoebottom remembers the clash well. 'Leeds were winning handsomely and Mick took the ball and went between the two Hull second rowers and split them like a pea pod, he didn't have to because the match was won and they both wanted to kill him but it didn't happen. Alan Preece was the same when he was at Hunslet, he once said to me before a game at Parkside, "I'm going to have that brother of yours", and afterwards he just came over in the bar and said, "I couldn't bloody catch him", and he was a hard man was "Moosey", but that was Mick's character.'

Two dazzling touchdowns in a twelve-try, 50-point thrashing of Doncaster were tempered by the loss of Mick's partner-in-crime Seabourne with an arm injury which necessitated Mick moving to his old role at scrum-half, but this only served to increase his dominance in proceedings. He was Man of the Match in a surprise defeat at Workington, no mean feat after Syd Hynes' revelations. 'We roomed together regularly for away games and we used to get up to some stuff on and off the field. We looked after each other and everyone else in the team if anyone was trying to take liberties. For that match at Workington just before Christmas in 1967, we stayed the night before in the Original Oak in Keswick. We thought we were invincible and we should have beaten them by about 50 points, but we'd been out on the drink the night before; rum and black. Mick got over the try-line but dropped the ball and then he took a blow to the stomach and started throwing up – we thought he was seriously injured and coughing up blood but it was just the remnants of the night before. We got narrowly beaten and Roy Francis went absolutely berserk, but it was just the wake-up call we needed.

Three Doncaster players attempt to hold Mick up just short of the line during a 50-0 Headingley rout on 16 December 1967.

Mick was just a great guy to have with you, he burned up energy and you wondered where it all came from. It would have been nice to have had a little of the stamina he seemed to have left towards the end of a gruelling game.'

Shoey orchestrated a late rally that saw off Wakefield at Headingley on Boxing Day – 'never at a loss for finding some new way to plague the life out of Trinity's defence' said the reports – before making light of the cloying Clarence Street mud to help destroy York 33-0 which included another beguiling brace of tries. Legendary England and Yorkshire cricketer Freddie Trueman reported on the match for the *Sunday People* and was unstinting in his praise. 'My toast to the New Year is Mick Shoebottom – the Leeds scrum-half who made this one-sided match worth watching', he began. 'He was elected Player of the Match by referee Thompson of Huddersfield – and for once I'm in full agreement with the man in charge. The stocky, fair-haired half-back, who was seriously bothered with injuries last season, proved he is back to his rip-roaring best. He took to the mud like a duck to water, scoring two tries and making three more. And he was over the line for what should have been a deserved hat-trick, but the touchdown was disallowed. However, Mick's thirty-seventh minute try, which covered the whole length of the field, was the high-spot of the match. He brought the ball out of defence, passed to centre Hynes and was up in support to take the return just over the half-way line. Then nobody could catch him.'

1968 was welcomed in with repeat fixtures against the Hull clubs with Leeds completing the double over both. Another two tries disposed of the Airlie Birds as Leeds took their points tally to 178 in seven matches, the last three of which saw them concede not a single try, but the best was yet to come. The match against Rovers was a hasty rearrangement owing to Headingley's under-soil heating after Leeds' game at St Helens and Hull Kingston Rovers' planned visit to Keighley had been called off due to heavy frost on top of snow. There was little between the sides in the standings, the Loiners second with 34 points from 22 games and the visitors third on the ladder, a point behind but with a match in hand. The Robins' last defeat, eight games previously, had been at home to Leeds and though they competed well, they were never a match for a side that, by general consensus, reached a new level for teamwork and the ability to keep the ball moving in mesmerizing fashion. Mick and his opposite number, Roger Millward, were cautioned in a fiery duel and although Shoey eventually limped off with a sprained ankle late on, his try from 30 yards out after eight men had handled had secured the spoils. In becoming the first side to score six tries in a match against Rovers for three years, Leeds' display won universal acclaim. Under the headline 'Title-chasing Leeds look like world-beaters', Jack Paul called it 'impeccable and impressive', and Shoey 'flawless', while Jack Nott commented that their play was, 'liberally laced with superb, sophisticated football' and Arthur Haddock said it 'was their peak performance…an unsurpassed brand of football'. Not surprisingly, perfectionist coach Francis disagreed. 'Obviously I was happy about our performance', he said, before ominously adding, 'But a number of things still need improving.' The most prophetic words, though, came from Paul Harrison when he began his report, 'Put your money on Leeds for the Rugby League Cup.' Tactically, Roy Francis' astuteness was beginning to pay off, as Barry Seabourne recalls. 'He developed an arrow format both left and right to give his half-backs maximum options to strike and to get the ball wider, quicker. The linking in of the likes of Ray Batten and Bev Risman to create the extra man on either side was crucial. The other thing about Roy's plan was that everyone had to know it, we only really had positions for kick-offs, scrums and penalties. If you found yourself near the play-the-ball you were expected to jump in and keep things moving, it was all about creating time and space and then exploiting it with speed and constant support.'

In fact, Leeds were not to lose again in Championship football until the last match of the regular season on Easter Monday as they retained their League Leaders' Trophy by a 7-point margin. Mick missed the next match after the Hull Kingston Rovers mauling, his first absence in thirty-one consecutive appearances, but returned as the focus switched to the Challenge Cup, which had last sported blue and amber ribbons eleven years earlier. A perfunctory 23-12 victory over Liverpool in the opening round, which included Mick claiming a try, came in the middle of an astonishing run which saw Leeds keep their try-line intact in thirteen out of nineteen league and cup clashes spread over a four month period. Indeed, City's two touchdowns – coupled with a later brace by Halifax at Thrum Hall – were the only three-pointers Leeds conceded in nine matches as spring beckoned. Bramley were summarily dispatched in round two as thoughts turned to the international arena. Mick's absence from the Yorkshire ranks, he had only appeared as a substitute against Cumberland at Castleford, had confounded many but by early February he was named as one of the shadow replacements for the Great Britain side to face France in Paris. Before the return game against the French at Odsal, and in preparation for the up-and-coming World Cup to be held in the Antipodes, the GB management decided to undertake one-off matches against club sides to act as tour trials. Two days after the Bramley cup tie and on the Monday before the return clash with the 'Chanticleers', Leeds took their turn under the Headingley lights and although defeated 25-7 in a fine, ultra competitive hit out, Mick did his future chances no harm with another sterling display, principally opposing and out-playing Roger Millward who was withdrawn at half-time, and that despite initially being ruled out of the contest after his weak ankle had swollen up again over the weekend and which eventually forced him off before the end. Arthur Haddock noted, 'Shoebottom enhanced his claim for a World Championship place. First at scrum-half, and then at off-half, he got through a remarkable amount of work.' Although the selectors opted for an unchanged line-up for the return match with the French, for the first time since 1961, calls from various quarters were growing for Shoey to be on the plane to Australia this time. Respected former player, coaching guru and current Bradford Northern manager Albert Fearnley pleaded with those in charge to pick players with personality and character as well as ability to make the trip, singling out Price (Bradford), Newell (Dewsbury), Hollindrake (Bramley), Shoebottom (Leeds), Hepworth (Castleford), Mantle (St Helens) and Dixon (Halifax) as his favourites. In trade paper the *Rugby Leaguer* readers' letters regularly suggested the same thing. G. Fletcher of Salford insisted that, 'Bob Burdell is the best hooker in the league. He should have been in the team long ago. Others are: Fletcher (Oldham), Bryant (Castleford) and Shoebottom (Leeds). If they want to win the World Cup they have to play these four.' Similarly, P.W. Harper, based at the Cambridge Hotel in Blackpool, included Mick in his eighteen-man squad, noting 'each of these players is fast, versatile, determined and well versed in the arts of rugby.' When the initial shortlist of twenty-four names was revealed by the Rugby Football League soon afterwards there was quiet satisfaction for Mick to find his name included alongside Roger Millward and Tommy Bishop of St Helens for the half-back slots, but there could be no complacency as Chapeltown Road made it clear the travelling number would eventually have to be reduced to nineteen.

Two key games in the space of four days in mid-March kept the Loiners' hopes of a first ever double on track. Oldham were summarily dispatched 13-0 at the Watersheddings in the third round of the Challenge Cup before revenge was gained at Knowsley Road for defeat in the first home league game of the season, Leeds confirming their place in the top four as a minimum and extinguishing St Helens' hopes of finishing top of the pile to boot. With Wigan coach and captain Eric Ashton in the stands, spying prior to the sides' meeting in the cup semi-final, Leeds were in command throughout against Saints, Mick scorching through from Barry Seabourne's reverse pass just before half-time to set up a worthy victory. Harold Mather said of the Leeds half-back combination, 'it was from their brainwork and fleetness of foot that some of their team's better attacks were developed.' The following weekend Leeds all but wrapped up the League Leaders' accolade with a resounding win at Featherstone and faced a week off before the eagerly awaited cup clash with Wigan – with the words of their coach ringing in their ears, 'Now we step up the work', announced Roy Francis, 'the lads are running into peak fitness and I don't want them to lose their edge. The only problem I should have is who to leave out.'

If the impressive win over Hull Kingston Rovers at Headingley in the title race had opened people's eyes as to the style of rugby Leeds were capable of serving up, then the comprehensive defeat of Wigan at Station Road, Swinton, in front of over 30,000 fans and sending the Loiners to Wembley set a new benchmark. With the World Cup party due to be confirmed the following Wednesday the match was important for Mick and he did not disappoint in a team performance that must rank as one of the finest demonstrated by men in blue and amber. Despite conceding an early penalty to Colin Tyrer, the Headingley men were dominant with Shoey at the hub of their expansive, electrifying attack. John Atkinson's seemingly effortless glide to the posts set them on their way and although Billy Boston powered through four would-be tacklers and looked a certain scorer in reply, he lost the ball over the try-line and Wigan's chance had gone. From Bernard Watson's forty-sixth minute interception try it was all Leeds as they crossed for three more glorious touchdowns, Mick heavily involved in the one for Syd Hynes as the vital link following another searing burst from Bill Ramsey – exemplifying the Hunslet born combination. Francis' vision of 'total football' had never been better illustrated and although the hardest of taskmasters, he was clearly delighted by the performance. 'Our last try crystallized everything I'd striven for', he said, 'perfection on a football field. Barry Seabourne scored from half-way with five colleagues in support and not an opponent in sight.' Naturally, Mick was one of them. For winger Alan Smith, it was the culmination of what had been brewing. 'We were on a roll, we were coming together, and the foundation for our success was there. That semi-final was almost the confirmation in our own minds as individuals that the team was bonded into a unit.' Journalist Phil King called it 'a staggering and supremely confident display' while Arthur Haddock noted that 'there was a distinct difference in class as Leeds coolly whipped Wigan 25-4 ... In technique and teamwork, in speed of thought and execution, Leeds had been vastly superior.' For the defeated Eric Ashton, there was no doubt where the game was won and lost. 'They were a better side and played good football. I have the highest opinion of half-backs Shoebottom and Seabourne, they are the best club pair in the league.' He continued: 'Not only are they good players, but they work splendidly together, and that is the important thing. They were the men who cut us up.' As Leeds Secretary Bill Carter looked forward to making the arrangements for Wembley, he was congratulated by the Wigan officials, who added to the accolades. 'In that period of the late '60s, we played what we all referred to at the club as "champagne rugby". After the 1968 Cup semi-final victory over Wigan, their Chairman came up to me and said about Mick, "By golly, you've got a wonderful player there."' John Atkinson picks it out as a landmark performance. 'Every so often in your career there's a match when everything seems to go right and that was the case at Swinton. For a coach, Roy must have sat there and thought 'this is perfection' and it virtually was. We were playing in an era where we probably didn't get the credit the performance actually deserved. Wigan didn't play badly that day but we just hit an absolute high. The fitness and ability all came together that day, everything that Roy had been trying came to fruition, it all clicked.'

Mick was at work when the news was broken to him of his inclusion as one of three new caps in the Great Britain World Cup squad to travel to the Antipodes, hooker Kevin Ashcroft of Leigh and Wakefield's Bob Haigh being the others. 'I'm flabbergasted', he was quoted as saying. 'I thought my career was over last season when a concrete beam fell on my back, but I have made a good recovery and have almost completed my four ambitions. I wanted to turn

The Leeds directors notify Mick of his World Cup selection.

out for Yorkshire and Great Britain, play at Wembley, and earn a trip to Australia.' The following week Leeds equalled the club record of eighteen consecutive wins when they beat Huddersfield before their delighted fans at Headingley, who had already seen Rugby League Council chairman John Smallwood of Keighley present skipper and fellow tourist Mick Clark with the League Leaders' and Yorkshire League Trophies. Clark is unequivocal in his assessment of Mick's worth at that time. 'He was just a young whippersnapper – full of it, full of energy and go. He brought a lot of humour to the dressing room, he was one of those "Jack the lad" type of characters who was always nobbling. He was the same in every game he played, all go all the time. Mick was the finest all-rounder I ever came across, whether playing in attack or defence. His positional play, his passing and tackling, and flair for the unexpected and the half-opening, put his stamp on every game. He was a dedicated player, never missed a training session, a social evening, or anything to do with the game and he never fell out with anybody. He was the backbone of the Leeds side, I really mean that.'

Wembley fever, where, ironically, Wakefield again stood in the path of Shoey's first winner's medal, was put on hold for the top sixteen Championship play-offs. He was inspirational with two tries, taking him to a season's tally of twenty, as Widnes were accounted for at home in a thrilling encounter, a clash that opposing captain Ray French remembers well. 'We were winning comfortably in the early stages and there was still nothing in it at half-time. Our side was full of young kids coming through like Ray Dutton, George Nicholls, Eric Hughes, Mal Aspey and when we got in the tiny, cramped dressing rooms in the old pavilion at the break one of our directors, Batty Foran, the local bookmaker in Widnes, was in there and called me over. "Ray" he said, "£50 a man if you win this game, tell the lads." Well that was a lot of money in those days, Widnes were on £22 for a victory in this first round of the Premiership. I asked him if he was sure and he just kept repeating "£50 a man" so I called the lads in and told them the new terms and that we had to win. Anyway we came out and lined up as Leeds were kicking off and I was guarding the touchline. Just as I was about to receive the ball I felt this tug on my jersey and it was Batty who had rushed down from the director's box and he's saying to me in a loud whisper, "I've made a mistake, it was £50 for the team, go and tell them quickly." Anyhow by then the ball had sailed over my head and into touch and Leeds never looked back. Mick scored a couple of tries and ran really well.' However, Roy Francis' desire for cup glory saw his side bow out of the double chase five days later when Wigan gained their revenge, also at Headingley.

That defeat gave Francis' side two-and-a-half weeks to prepare for the Cup Final while their opponents gained maximum confidence by retaining their Championship crown. Francis was aware of the possibility of external distractions and looked to keep them to a minimum although a 'Variety Club of Great Britain' commemorative lunch at the Queen's Hotel shared with Leeds United was eagerly attended, Mick never having lost his affection for the round ball game.

The 1968 Challenge Cup Final will always be remembered for the wrong reasons, its notoriety arising from freak weather conditions. Torrential rain in the lead up to kick-off and continuing during the action caused the match to become a near farce rather than the hoped for spectacle between two of the code's finest exponents. Whilst it should have made household names of a host of the most talented players of a generation, it unfairly reduced Trinity's Lance Todd Trophy winner Don Fox to the role of pantomime villain. Leeds

Championship play-off in 1968, Widnes forwards French and Davies are powerless to stop Mick reaching the whitewash.

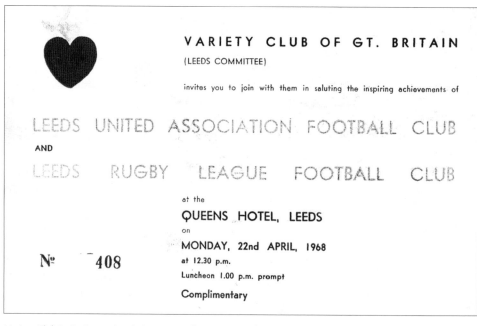

Variety Club invitation as the city's sporting elite come together.

prepared well in the lead up to the game as Barry Seabourne recalls. 'I felt that even though we triumphed in bizarre circumstances, it was a final we deserved to win. At Crystal Palace the day before we had the most superb training session; it was all quality work, like a racehorse priming itself just before the Derby, and we just knew that we weren't going to lose. You only needed to look at the way we demolished Wigan in the semi-final to see what a good side we were. Roy had this passionate desire to win the Cup because he had come so close before with Hull. I fell out with him a bit because I thought that we were good enough to do the double that year, but before Wembley, in the championship play-offs, he rested some of the players and we were beaten by Wigan. The Final shouldn't have gone ahead. We were ready to play but the match really should have been replayed as it came down purely to mistakes and the awarding of a try on both sides that never was. It was tremendous drama but there were so many great players who weren't given a real chance to show what they could do.' As BBC commentator Eddie Waring – who immortalized the denouement with his apt and often-quoted commentary 'He's missed it, he's missed it the poor lad' – put it in his column for the *Sunday Mirror* the following day, 'Master of suspense Alfred Hitchcock couldn't have produced a more dramatic or sensational finish.'

Despite finishing the season at the top of the league, Leeds were perceived to be the un-fancied side.' They were waved off from Headingley on the Thursday for their base at the National Recreation Centre by a handful of fans, friends and family – Mick's young daughter Amanda amongst them – and someone must have known something as a toy duck in the club colours hung from the roof just inside the door of the coach. According to Arthur Haddock, who accompanied the team, the squad was apprehensive about their 'new' base but they need not have worried. 'It became the unanimous opinion of the players that they couldn't have had a better spot to wind up their preparation' he diarized. 'The food was splendid and generously served...among a husky set of chaps who themselves are rather good with a knife and fork in their hands.' Relaxation that evening was undertaken with a trip to the London Palladium to see Tom Jones in concert followed by Francis taking his charges to the top floor of the prestigious Hilton Hotel for a panoramic view of the capital by night.

Seabourne's recollection of the intensity of the final training session is borne out by Haddock. 'As to the training pitch, this was first class...and some of the Southerners, mostly soccer adherents, who watched the last work-out of the Leeds boys must have had their eyes opened at the extent to which Roy Francis put his charges "through the mill". One felt that when Roy finally called "that will do" that Leeds were not going to lack stamina. I've watched a few teams train at Wembley in my forty years as a scribe, but none ever worked harder than this Leeds outfit. They romped up and down the practice arena for an hour – and woe betide anyone who showed the slightest sign of easing up!' He was later to give an insight into how Mick struggled to cope with the pressure of playing in his first really big game. 'There is a popular belief that nothing can disturb the equilibrium of a footballer and he goes into a match as if it were just a practice session. This image of a professional performer was particularly vivid in the case of Mick Shoebottom. Most people imagined he was impervious to nerves simply because as soon as he felt the turf under his feet he became transformed, always on the go, eager to be in the thick of the action. Yet Mick, a wholehearted player who tackled anything in sight and never shirked striding into the thinnest opening, was human like the rest of us and certainly had his "nerves". The lad who used to sit up front in the

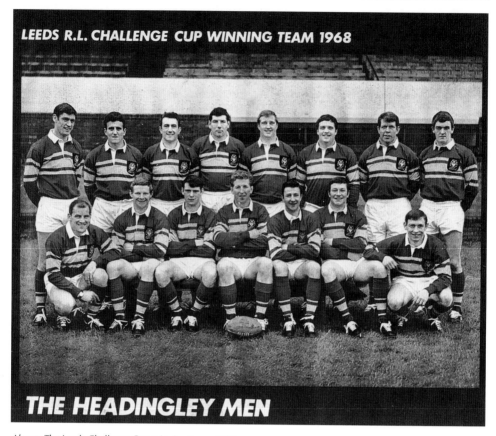

LEEDS R.L. CHALLENGE CUP WINNING TEAM 1968

THE HEADINGLEY MEN

Above: The Leeds Challenge Cup winning team, 1968.

Opposite: Taken from the brochure supplied to all the players taking part in the 1968 Challenge Cup Final.

motor coach, rarely far from John Atkinson, was a very different sight from the spring-heeled half-back who, once a game got going, became a veritable fireball. The sixty minutes before a big game were agony to Shoey; you could see him going through Hell, and it made you feel for the poor lad. On the way to Wembley the usually jaunty Mick could hardly be consoled, he was holding his head in his hands and in such a state of tension that one imagined he would be unable to snap out of it and play his normal game. Shoey invariably contrived to pull himself together and when you saw him rubbing his hands and doing a spot of high-stepping after the team had trotted out, it was all part of his routine towards regaining composure and balance.'

The rain and strong wind began in earnest before kick-off that Friday. Although the downpour left a few standing pools of water – despite the ground staff's attempts to pitchfork it away – RFL officials, the police and referee John Hebblethwaite of York deemed that with 87,000 people already in or around the ground, and the match the centrepiece of the afternoon's broadcast output, the show had to go on. According to Alan Smith, the Leeds players were not unduly concerned by the elements. 'We were confident going into the Final,

THE RUGBY FOOTBALL LEAGUE

Patron :
HER MAJESTY THE QUEEN

President :
The Right Hon. THE EARL OF DERBY, M.C.

CHALLENGE CUP COMPETITION

FINAL TIE

LEEDS

v

WAKEFIELD TRINITY

on

SATURDAY, 11th MAY, 1968

KICK-OFF at 3.0 p.m.

at

THE EMPIRE STADIUM, WEMBLEY

Programme of Arrangements

W. FALLOWFIELD, O.B.E..
Secretary.

Wakefield were just putting a new team together themselves and we thought that they were just off their peak after ten great years; we really thought it was going to be our day. Shoey just ignored the weather and went out and tackled them even if it meant him having to slide for 20 yards.' Mick's walk out into the arena in the middle of the Leeds line seemed a little tentative, head bowed throughout the stride to the centre for the ceremonial presentations. The opening fourteen minutes saw the sides trade penalties, Bev Risman putting Leeds 4-2 ahead before the effect of the weather came into play. Don Fox kicked for touch and John Atkinson aquaplaned over the touchline without the ball, leaving Wakefield winger Ken Hirst to retain his balance, hack on and claim the try which Fox converted to put the favourites 7-4 up. Atkinson's anguish was clearly evident as he hammered the ball down the tunnel in disgust. Then the rains really came, accompanied by thunder, lightning and hailstones to produce an almost surreal backdrop as the players struggled to keep their feet and brought up huge plumes of water with every tackle or collision. Unsurprisingly, the next score did not materialize until the sixty-ninth minute – and it was one of the most contentious in the history of the sport. Risman's long-clearing punt stuck in one of the pools of water, Atkinson got to the ball first and hacked on over the Trinity line as Poynton, Hirst, Batty and Coetzer converged on him. With Atkinson blocked from getting to the ball, referee Hebblethwaite stunned the watching crowd by awarding a penalty try which Risman converted. Eddie Waring noted that the 'Trinity players were flabbergasted but there was little or no protest.' Two minutes from time, Leeds were awarded a long-range penalty with skipper Mick Clark imploring Risman to kick the ball dead at the very least to keep Wakefield pinned near their own line. The kick was almost too good as it torpedoed through the posts to make it 11-7 but gave Wakefield one last chance to salvage the match from the kick-off on half way. The restart bounced uncontrollably off the boot of Bernard Watson and Hirst, haring up the middle, toed the ball forward and just out-sprinted a desperate Shoey in the race to claim what should have been the decisive try. The rest is rugby folklore. Mick was one of several Leeds players who stared straight-ahead while Don Fox teed up the kick which could have given his side the double, before his almost delirious leap of delight when he realized the ball had skidded off the side of the luckless kicker's boot – signalling the start of many Loiners fans' celebrations, the whistle going immediately afterwards.

John Atkinson will never forget the mixed emotions conjured up by the extraordinary sequence of events. 'Had the Final been a dry day it would have been a classic because Wakefield were such a good side. Mick wasn't bothered by the conditions; he just got on the rugby field and any other problems or concerns he might have had just disappeared. It was as if he was made to be there. That's how he treated everything to do with rugby and he played with such a smile on his face. We were all still pretty young at Wembley and although everyone remembers Don Fox we were just so overjoyed because we'd just won the Rugby League Challenge Cup. We got out of jail obviously, we very much appreciated that but not at that particular minute. The Final was the accumulation of all the good rugby that we had been putting together and here we were succeeding on the big stage. As daft as it sounds, despite the conditions, we didn't know how to play any other way. I made a terrible mistake trying to keep the ball in play chasing back only to give Kenny Hirst a free run to the line. Common sense would tell you in the wet just to leave it but that wasn't how we played at the time, my idea was to keep it in the field of play, pick it up and run back at them because

Mick and John Atkinson down Harold Poynton at Wembley.

Mick watches Ray Batten fling out a trademark pass in the Watersplash decider.

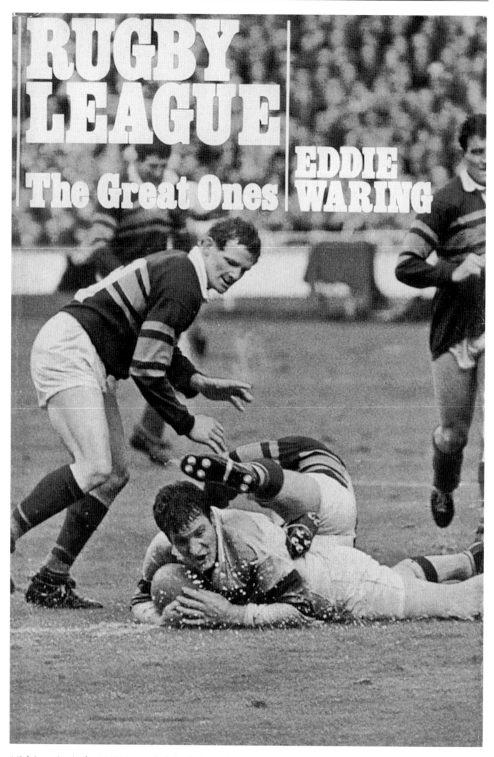

Mick in action in the 1968 Watersplash final, the perfect cover for Eddie Waring's book *The Great Ones*, published the following year.

From left to right: John Atkinson, skipper Mick Clark, Bev Risman and a grinning Shoey on the lap of honour at Wembley in 1968.

that was what was natural to us. Next thing I know I'm sat on the railings and they're coming past and scoring but we couldn't change our style. Besides, if I'd let the ball go into touch, Trinity would have had head and feed at the scrum and our forwards would have played hell with me.' Of all the opinions penned about this quite astonishing game, feature writer Robin Marlar's was perhaps the most poignant. 'Men and ball glissaded out of control. All the plans of coaches, all the evident skill of the individuals were brought to nothing. The match became a lottery. But what a thrilling one! In the first half, when conditions were at their best, Leeds produced hints of the polish that has earned them such respect all season.' Of the defining finale he wrote, 'Fox … sliced the ball off the edge of his boot and sank to the ground like a stricken bull. But though we bled for him, justice perhaps did not. A final, and I regret, most critical word about the Lance Todd Trophy. Voting takes place ten minutes before the end and minds are no doubt made up even before that: thirteen to Fox, eight to Risman – a bad decision which was the only real blot in an otherwise wonderful and memorable afternoon.' But even then fickle fate saw Leeds have the last laugh as Trinity's Neil Fox was forced to withdraw from captaining the World Cup squad through injury, Atkinson being drafted in as his replacement and Risman taking over the captaincy.

Shoey's characteristic smile in the foreground, next to John Atkinson with his arm raised, as Mick Clark gets chaired with the Challenge Cup.

Jubilation was tempered with relief as Mick received his cherished medal from the Duke of Kent and did the customary lap of honour. After riotous celebrations in the North dressing room, the Leeds party decamped to the Park Lane Hotel for a commemorative gala dinner. After the hors d'oeuvres, Dover sole was accompanied by a 1964 bottle of Pouilly-Fuisse, the Aylesbury duck was washed down with a 1962 Beaune, and Moet and Chandon Dry Imperial champagne was the perfect accompaniment to the Baked Alaska with cherries. Interspersed with frequent visits to the bar, Chairman Alfred Sharman toasted the Queen and responded to the Lord Mayor of Leeds, Colonel Lawrence Turnbull's eulogy to the club and its standing in the community before skipper Mick Clark closed the formal proceedings. An executive of the hotel later wrote to Mr Sharman to say that his charges were the best behaved players of any football team to have stayed there, although for John Atkinson the event meant less to the players than perhaps it should have done. 'The celebrations were quite muted because we were in the wrong place, they didn't want us there really and it was all a bit staid and old fashioned for us. The bar closed at eleven o'clock and there was only one lady serving everybody. There were so many people at the dinner from all walks of life, the BBC and Members of Parliament; we had better occasions when we got beaten.'

The sun, of course, shone the following day; the Leeds entourage greeted by massive cheering crowds as their victory parade wended its way to the Civic Hall for another champagne reception. Rather than the more traditional open-topped double-decker bus, the players crammed into a coach and removed the plastic sun roofs to squeeze out of the top, four at a time, like the objects in a coconut shy. Shoey stationed himself right at the front, grasping the silverware in concert with Mick Clark but the two were quickly swapping their Leeds blazers for the suits of the national side, in dapper dark grey worsted Terylene which were manufactured in the city by Hepworth's tailoring. According to John Atkinson, they were not as functional as they might have first appeared. 'I was a late replacement for the '68 World Cup squad, as much for that semi-final performance as anything else. It was the first time I'd been away from home for any length of time but it gave me the chance to see Shoey in his entirety, he was up for everything. It was a bit like putting a child in charge of a sweet shop and saying "look just please yourself". He loved everything about being away on tour. The preparations, though, were horrendous. We had suits that would have been fit to go to Russia in because they were that big, thick and warm; white lycra-looking tracksuits which made some of the forwards look something like circus elephants and we were given two bri-nylon, drip-dry shirts that made your neck red and everybody sweat. Everybody stunk and we were followed by flies for miles. They made us wear them on the plane journey over but you weren't bothered because you were there on tour but we weren't a particularly good side when you analyse it.'

A hectic week of interviews and photo-shoots at Headingley coupled with a few light training sessions followed – the last at the *Yorkshire Evening Post*'s Glen Road Sports Ground where the squad was offered a £250 per man bonus if they retained the trophy won by Eric

Mick celebrates winning the 1968 Challenge Cup Final at Wembley with his early mentor, Loiners' esteemed coach Roy Francis.

PARK LANE HOTEL

LEEDS RUGBY LEAGUE
FOOTBALL CLUB

DINNER

LEEDS v. WAKEFIELD TRINITY

SATURDAY, 11th MAY, 1968

The Rugby League
Challenge Cup Final
at Wembley

Above: A triumphant return to Leeds with the Challenge Cup.

Opposite: The 1968 Leeds *v.* Wakefield Trinity dinner menu.

Ashton's men on home soil some eight years before. It was generally felt that the British Selectors had 'played it safe' with their nineteen choices, having already dismantled the side after their third consecutive Ashes series loss in the winter of 1967. Skipper Bev Risman was delighted that Shoey was amongst them. 'He was always the life and soul. He wasn't a great comedian but he had this ability to laugh at himself and be the centre of the joke especially if he was going on about his prowess. He took the Mickey-taking in his stride totally, gave as good as he got and kept coming back for more. He was so easy to captain, a true model professional. He never argued with anybody and just got on with doing exactly what it was he was required to do.'

Coach Colin Hutton and Manager Bill Fallowfield's major concern, despite the trial matches and regular training get-togethers during the season, was lack of preparation time; the party were flying out on Saturday 18 May and due to play their first game against the much fancied hosts at the Sydney Cricket Ground only a week later. An arduous 'promotional' tour of Queensland had been added to the schedule and whilst that would have made an ideal springboard those games were instead tagged on at the end. The tourists were based at the Olympic Hotel, literally a stone's throw from the venue of the opening game with the players' balconies overlooking the famous stadium. Training, which took place at the front of the hotel, was necessarily light after the long, draining thirty-six-hour flight and interspersed with numerous official functions at the various Leagues' clubs, a heady cocktail, especially for the newcomers to touring like Mick and Widnes back-rower Ray French, now the voice of BBC TV's Rugby League coverage. He recalls in his book *My Kind of Rugby*, 'This was hardly the correct preparation for a game of such stature. The party had insufficient time to socialize and live with each other, and insufficient time to recognize each other's faults and qualities.

Solid, honest-to-goodness Englishmen in the shape of Mick Shoebottom, Cliff Watson and Arnie Morgan helped to mould the party, but it was to take time, and a week was not enough. The social life was hectic in that first week in Sydney and came as a shock to many of us. Many of the players, led by an Australian tycoon known affectionately as "Last Card" Louie (on account of his huge winnings on the turn of a playing card), were introduced to the delights of the "Pink Pussy Club" and were wined and dined at every opportunity.

Shoey, Mick Clark and Great Britain skipper Bev Risman measure each other up for their Lions attire.

The 1968 World Cup party with those suits! Left to right are: Tommy Bishop (St Helens), Roger Millward (Hull K.R.), Derek Edwards (Castleford), Peter Flanagan (Hull K.R.), Bev Risman (Leeds) captain, Colin Hutton (Hull K.R.) trainer-coach, Kevin Ashcroft (Leigh), Alan Burwell (Hull K.R.), Chris Young (Hull K.R.), Mick Shoebottom (Leeds), Ian Brooke (Wakefield Trinity), Clive Sullivan (Hull), Arnold Morgan (Featherstone Rovers), Bob Haigh (Wakefield Trinity), John Atkinson (Leeds), Cliff Watson (St Helens), Charlie Renilson (Halifax), Mr John Smallwood (Keighley), chairman of the R.L. Council, John Warlow (St Helens), Mick Clark (Leeds), Ray French (Widnes), and Mr W. Fallowfield team manager.

The 1968 Great Britain party pose before flying out to Australia and New Zealand. From left to right, back row: C. Sullivan, B. Haigh, J. Warlow, C. Watson, R. French, M. Clark, A. Morgan, M. Shoebottom, K. Ashcroft, C. Young. Front row: C. Renilson, I. Brooke, P. Flanagan, Mr W. Fallowfield (team manager), N. Fox, C. Hutton, R. Millward, B. Risman, A. Burwell. Kneeling: T. Bishop and D. Edwards.

The squad relaxes at Brisbane's Lone Pine Koala Sanctuary.

Above: The Lions take their first look at the infamous Sydney Cricket Ground.

Opposite: Mick makes the cover of *Rugby League Pictorial*, June 1968.

Above all, even when socializing, the Aussies made no bones about their desire to beat us…wherever we were there was no escape from the World Cup.' Ray confirmed that Mick was invariably amongst those who frequented the club, adding 'The Olympic wasn't one of those big posh hotels, it was basically a rough, old-fashioned Sydney pub with rooms but the camaraderie and craic was what really made it and Mick was always at the heart of it. If you wanted to make up a party of four or five – say me, Cliff Watson, John Warlow, Mick Clark – to go out for the night he would always be a part of it. Or if there was a boat trip on the harbour or to the koala sanctuary in Brisbane, he'd be the first there.'

RUGBY LEAGUE *PICTORIAL*

Vol. 1 — No. 5   JUNE, 1968   PRICE: 20c

THIRD FLOOR, ASTON HOUSE, 297 ELIZABETH STREET, SYDNEY. 2000   •   PHONE 798 6517, 61 2623

A dramatic action shot of England's centre, Mike Shoebottom, as Johnny Greaves goes low in the World Cup clash at Sydney Cricket Ground.

There was also the feeling that the Lions were handicapped by a conservative team selection, eschewing power and aggression in the pack and looking for an uneasy compromise of styles in the backs. It meant that although Mick proudly gained his first cap – along with Bob Haigh – it was in the unfamiliar position of centre, Roger Millward and Tommy Bishop forming the half-back combination. He said of his selection with typical bravado, 'I know stand-off is my club place but I prefer centre', and certainly the Aussies billed the contest as 'our forwards against their backs', the Sydney newspapers commenting, 'The British backs are exceptionally smart. From skipper Risman's brainy play at full-back to fiery Bishop at scrum-half Britain have speed and experience. Centres Burwell and Shoebottom, a rugged stand-off with Leeds, are capable of cracking the toughest defence.'

Unfortunately, in front of a fanatical near-capacity crowd of just over 62,000 basking in unseasonably warm conditions, it did not turn out that way. Before the game, while somewhat bizarrely thirty-seven-year-old Lewis Jones was leading his Wentworthville side to a 12-10 victory over Universities in a curtain raiser, the Great Britain players were being lectured by New Zealand referee John Percival on his expectations at the play-the-ball. His pedantic interpretation and constant penalizing of the Lions went some way to determine the outcome. Aussie new boy Eric 'Ecka' Simms kicked eight goals in a 25-10 success, although it was the class of loose forward Johnny Raper, who scored the crucial try late on, which proved to be the real difference. Mick's contribution was mixed, always looking to impose himself on the opposition although suffering from mounting frustration, one of the successful penalties being awarded after he had been deemed guilty of a late tackle by the touch judge. Jack McNamara's match report said, 'The tackling generally was sound although Mick Shoebottom did not look happy in the centre', although the usually vituperative Australian press were somewhat kinder. 'England [*sic*] tried hard to get back in the game through Ray French and a gentleman with the curious name of Shoebottom. Shoebottom, a centre, finished the match with the "tough guy" tag. Mr Percival cautioned him twice near the finish.' Both men were dropped for the crucial second match a week later in Auckland against France, Mick making way for club mate John Atkinson to win his first cap.

Before they left for the land of the long white cloud, the British party licked their wounds during another round of functions which included being guests of honour at a top Sydney store which was holding a 'Britain '68' exhibition. They were also rigorously put through their paces by Colin Hutton in training, with special attention paid to rectifying the penalties they had conceded principally at the play-the-ball, the weather in Sydney turning distinctly blustery during the session. Incessant rain greeted them on arrival in New Zealand on the following Tuesday for a must-win game, threatening to turn the notoriously muddy Carlaw Park pitch – where the French had already upset the Kiwis – into a quagmire. Mick's spirit, despite his disappointment at being dropped, and an indication of the squad's general camaraderie, was illustrated when he and twenty-one-year-old John Atkinson spent the day before the big game doing the side's laundry at their hotel after 'volunteering' for the job. 'We cannot guarantee that the kit will be spotless but we are doing our best', John shouted to reporters above the hum of the machines as he and Shoey toiled with a huge pile of muddy shorts and jerseys. He looks back on those domesticities now with a grin. 'We ended up washing everyone's kit and we got paid a few dollars for it in the end. Bill Fallowfield asked us what we were doing and we mentioned that no one had washed any of it since we had

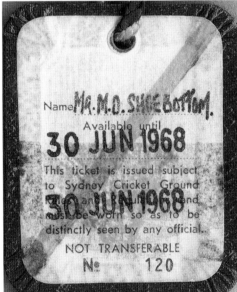

Top left: The Leeds contingent, from left to right, John Atkinson, Mick and Bev Risman take a stroll around Auckland.

Top right and above left and right: Mick's momentoes from an unforgettable experience.

left home – and New Zealand was horrendous because it was thick with mud. We found a washing machine in the basement of the hotel and we started doing ours and the next thing you know it was, "will you do this, will you do these?" and suddenly there was this big pile of filthy, disgusting laundry beside us. The difference between that tour in '68 and the next one in '70 was that we were very much on our own.'

Although they may have looked the part, the Great Britain players again flattered to deceive on matchday as they failed to come to terms with the torrential rain and treacherous surface. Veteran French prop Georges Ailleres led his side in percentage, possession football in which they rarely made a mistake with Jean Capdouze peppering the British line with kicks until an inevitable mistake allowed winger Jean-Rene Ledru to gather and score the only try, Bev Risman and Roger Garrigues swapping penalties in a dour 7-2 defeat for the Lions. Australia's easy victory over New Zealand the day before meant that the last round of matches were purely academic, with the two unbeaten sides having already qualified for the Final, leaving Great Britain and New Zealand to fight it out at the Sydney Cricket Ground for the honour of avoiding the wooden spoon. Mick was recalled to the bench in a side that threw off its shackles to show the paltry 14,000 crowd what they were capable of. With Risman in commanding form, the British led 20-4 at half-time allowing the management the luxury of bringing off Roger Millward to give Shoey a run, his gratitude shown when he shot through a gap and cantered clear unchallenged for his first try in the national colours just after the break in what was ultimately a comfortable 38-14 win.

Mick came into his own on the trip up to Queensland and the arduous prospect of four matches in five days combined with more traditional sightseeing, sunbathing, swimming and grandiose official receptions. A sparkling carefree display saw off Toowoomba 28-10 in the opening clash, Mick kicking two conversions and a drop goal in the first half before moving from stand-off to scrum-half in the second where his competitive nature nearly landed him in trouble, as Jack McNamara reported in the *Sunday Observer*. 'Referee Leo Cronin often upset the tourists and there was one unpleasant incident in the second half. After he had penalized Britain, Shoebottom booted the ball away in annoyance. Cronin ordered him to retrieve it. As Shoebottom walked slowly to get the ball, Miller petulantly kicked it farther back. Shoebottom shaped as if to grab Miller who ducked smartly out of the way.'

Two days later Clive Sullivan's four tries helped defeat the Maroons at Lang Park with Mick an admiring spectator, and the next afternoon, amid ninety degree heat, the tourists faced North Queensland at the Townsville Sports Reserve in front of a huge carnival crowd, many of whom were farmers and miners who had trekked for miles through the outback to see the game. They were not disappointed. In a typically rugged first half which saw the scores locked at 2-2, Ray French picked out Mick's contribution; 'I can vividly remember that game. It was very, very hot, in fact at half-time all the players went under the showers in full kit and the team talk was done with us under the cold running water. By then the squad was battered and the management virtually looking for volunteers just to get a side out on the Park. It was rough, one of the hardest games because [North Queensland] had a lot of young lads who were looking to knock our heads off. Mick put his hand up to play at loose forward, and, although the call was just to get through the game unscathed, Mick actually relished it and was determined to give the impression that we were prepared for the fight, and he ripped into them right from the off. He sorted every one of them out; he was dropping forward after

A typical Aussie reception laid on for the tourists in Queensland.

forward and the crowd was growing increasingly restless at the physical nature of the way he played, and after about twenty-five minutes their forwards were hardly daring to run the ball at us. Eventually the referee pulled me to one side and said "Frenchy if you don't sort him out, he's marching, he's going." I had a quick word with Mick and he just said, "Forget it", then rolled up his sleeves and really got stuck in and managed to get through the game. He was that type of a guy; he would do anything for the cause or for his team-mates on the field. In the second half we had things all our own way, running in tries as we pleased because I think by then he had flattened the entire pack and they had all been substituted.' Mick scored one try and set up Bev Risman for another in a highly satisfying 25-2 success.

The following night, again in temperatures of over ninety degrees despite a ten o'clock kick-off, the tourists broke new ground when they maintained their unbeaten record against North West Queensland in the uncompromising mining town of Mount Isa, Mick lining up as a substitute after again volunteering to play to make up the numbers. Ray French described it in his book as, 'like playing in Dodge City and certainly Kitty McShane's saloon was no less rough when an after-match reception was held. Only a quick exit by many of the players allowed the timbers to stay up as many a young Aussie, bolstered to overflowing by beer, strutted up and down offering to take on all comers.'

The players returned to England via an unscheduled stopover in Hong Kong, explained by Ray French. 'The plane broke down and needed a special part to be flown out, and as there

Mick and Roger Millward are first to the bar.

Back at last, Ian Brooke and Mick show off their Kowloon fishing hats at Manchester Airport.

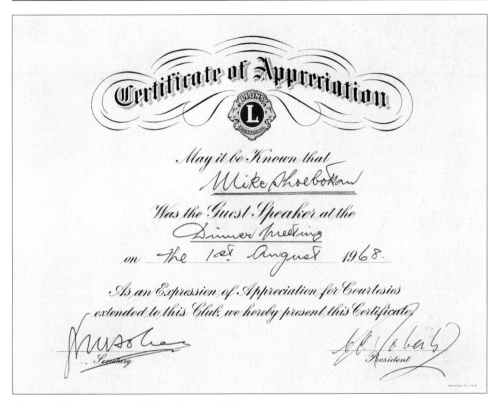

Certificate of Appreciation

May it be Known that

Mike Shoebottam

Was the Guest Speaker at the

Dinner meeting

on the 1st August 1968.

As an Expression of Appreciation for Courtesies extended to this Club, we hereby present this Certificate

_____
Secretary

_____
President

Dinner certificate awarded to Mick on 1 August 1968.

was no one to mend it, we had a week's extra holiday. We stayed at the Merlin Hotel and I remember going out in a rickshaw with Mick to see the sights. One day we went with John Warlow, who had done his national service with the Welsh Fusiliers, over to their barracks in the city and had a really good day out there. Mick was always up for a party and a laugh but when it came to playing rugby and he was alongside you, you had some ammunition.' The stopover explains why Mick and Wakefield three-quarter Ian Brooke arrived at Manchester's Ringway Airport sporting fetching straw fishermen's hats bought in Kowloon, but this was only part of the story of a convoluted return journey. The rest is related by John Atkinson. 'Mick actually sent all his clothes home from New Zealand because he'd bought a load of stuff and he couldn't get it all in his luggage so he sent his clothes on ahead. We got to Hong Kong and BOAC went on strike. We landed at the airport later than expected and that was it, we were only supposed to stay for a night but they left us there for nearly a week. We were based in Kowloon and the humidity was absolutely unbelievable and Mick just had his thick tour suit and one of those nylon shirts so he was going round trying to borrow t-shirts and all sorts of gear off people. Like touring squads do, we all told him to bugger off. We were taking the Mickey out of him for the entire time, telling him that he couldn't possibly be going out again in that smelly suit. They'd obviously got them cheap at the Rugby League, the badges on them were so heavy that they made you list to one side when you walked.

Arthur Crowther, the icon of kit men and a constant source of support and advice for Mick and his team mates, polishes the Yorkshire League trophy which the Joiners retained in 1967/68.

He was drenched in sweat the entire time we were there. When we came back to the UK we were stopped by customs, which is hardly surprising when you think what we'd got on us. Tommy Bishop was the first through and they asked him if he had anything to declare and he told them no. They then requested him to open up his suitcase and he got arrested and fined £70 for everything he'd brought back, which was a lot of money in those days. They eventually got to Michael and when they asked him to open his case these three sheepskin rugs came out like a snake uncoiling. The two customs officers looked at him in total disbelief and started searching for some kind of false platform in the bottom of his bag. They asked him where he'd been and he said, "I've been to Australia" with a smile, and then they wanted to know for how long and he replied, "seven weeks". They stared at him and just said "oh, right", folded up the rugs, struggled to close the case, gave it back to him and motioned him to go through. They must have thought he was a complete lunatic, but when he was involved in anything to do with rugby you couldn't stop him laughing. He had no hang-ups.'

7

1968/69
CHAMPIONS

Shoey, John Atkinson, Mick Clark and Bev Risman were not the only men from the Headingley camp who were in Australia during the summer of 1968, their efforts, if not successes, acknowledged by commemorative presentations from the Supporters' Club on their return. Innovative ARL founder club North Sydney, themselves perennial underachievers, had persuaded coach Roy Francis to take up a six week consultancy at their famous Oval after his triumph with Leeds. Not surprisingly, he made a significant impression on the Bears' players and management and it was not long before approaches were being made for him to join them on a full-time basis, as Ken Eyre recalls. 'Roy caused a lot of the interest in him at North Sydney deliberately; he went over there as a consultant first and told the media what he could do if he had access to their resources full-time and all about his training methods, so they made him an offer.' Understandable uncertainty faced the Loiners as they ran out for the new season, despite the record-breaking introduction of sixteen-year-old full-back John Holmes in the Lazenby Cup where he accumulated a seemingly nerveless 24 points on debut. A typically pugnacious performance from Alex Murphy scuppered the cup holders in the first championship match at Leigh, Mick darting over a fine solo try to no avail, but two days later Hull Kingston Rovers were beaten at Craven Park and, more significantly, St Helens – who had initially threatened to go on strike but were instead on a bonus of £25 per man – were outplayed in the first home match of the campaign, the third game in a hectic opening week.

September saw the start of the Yorkshire Cup and with Francis being pursued for a decision on his future; his charges looked to make a fitting on-field gesture to their mentor. Hull were the opening hurdle at the Boulevard and though influential scrum-half Chris Davidson only arrived minutes before the kick-off, causing extreme consternation in the home ranks, the hosts led 9-4 at the break. In the second half Leeds cut loose to register 26 unanswered points, Mick crowning a stunning win by twisting out of Clive Sullivan's tackle for the final try by the posts. The Loiners carried that swashbuckling form into the next league game against Warrington at Headingley, causing Jack Paul to report, 'If Leeds' coach Roy Francis decides – probably tomorrow – to accept the glittering offer from Australian club North Sydney, Headingley can at least be happy that he will leave them with one of the slickest outfits in the game. Leeds were more superior than the scoreline suggests. Stand-off Mike Shoebottom, scrum-half Barry

The four Leeds players who went on the 1968 World Cup tour, from left to right: Bev Risman, Mick Clark, Mick Shoebottom and John Atkinson are feted by club chairman Alfred Sharman and the Supporters' Club Queen.

Seabourne, centre Bernard Watson and their Leeds colleagues crossed the Warrington line ten times, only to have four of their efforts disallowed for hairline forward passes. Mistakes are inevitable the way Leeds run, handle and back up at top pace…But Leeds' football is exciting, exhilarating stuff, and I only wish there were even a dozen other teams who could emulate it.' A hard-fought win at Featherstone in the second round of the Yorkshire Cup, which saw Rovers unable to breach the Leeds try-line, followed, but injuries accentuated by midweek County Championship matches – for which Mick was initially named on the bench against both Cumberland and Lancashire but withdrew – saw him revert to scrum-half to oppose Alex Murphy in the return Championship clash with Leigh immediately prior to two cup ties in three days. Shoey was in imperious form, completely overshadowing his illustrious opponent and instigating waves of sweeping attacks, culminating in a wonderful 60-yard defence-splitting run in which he beat virtually all of the flailing Leigh defenders before sending in John Langley for his second try. He is another of Mick's contemporaries to hold the creative firebrand in the highest esteem. 'He was a great guy, one of the lads, and one of the best rugby players I have known. He and Syd looked after us, he was hard and he could give it as well as take it but he was a beautiful player as well. He was quick off the mark and he had fantastic hands. He was always 100 per cent although occasionally not in training mind you. Like Keith Hepworth he was naturally incredibly fit so they didn't need to train much. He'd always have a great excuse if needed for not doing this or doing that but come matchday he was always right on his game. We had a great team then but part of that was because we enjoyed ourselves together.'

Another touchdown, this time a controversial and crucial one, with Salford winger Paul Jackson and full-back Ken Gwilliam claiming to have ended Mick's breathless 70-yard run and slide for the corner just short, won a tense Floodlit Trophy clash before Halifax stood in the way of a Yorkshire Cup Final appearance. A third consecutive away draw meant the toughest of tasks at a rain-swept Thrum Hall, with the home side undefeated on their intimidating, sloping midden but Leeds' defensive qualities were to the fore in a tense 12-5 win. An emphatic defeat at St Helens, with Bev Risman commenting afterwards, 'Micks Clark and Shoebottom were the only forwards we had in the second half!', was hardly the ideal preparation to take on Castleford in the Yorkshire Cup decider especially as Shoey ended the Saints game limping out on the wing as a result of his assiduous efforts. Both sides lobbied for the Final to be played at Wakefield's Belle Vue ground, which suited Mick who lived nearby, and just over 12,500 fans saw Castleford searching for their initial County Cup triumph and Leeds their first in ten years. The contest failed to live up to the pre-match hype, the blue and ambers reverting to their Wembley line-up of five months before and posting two early tries never to be headed. Both were the result of Castleford errors, Mick on hand to sweep up a ball lost by Malcolm Reilly on his own quarter for Ken Eyre, Ray Batten and Albert Eyre to send in Alan Smith for the opening score and that set the tone. Mick competently shackled Castleford danger man, skipper Alan Hardisty, Jack Bentley noting in the *Daily Express* that he was, 'the iron-hand guardian of the Leeds middle'. Late on he produced one of his swinging trademark bursts through the cover before being brought down just short of glory. The trophy was the club's eighth in an overcrowded cabinet; joining the Lazenby Cup, Yorkshire League, League Leaders', Challenge Cup, Mackeson Trophy and at second team level, Yorkshire Senior Championship Shield and Yorkshire League Challenge Cup. For legendary bag and backroom man Arthur Crowther, an unsung hero of the support staff, it meant an endless round of polishing that he relished. 'I only wish I had a few more to clean', he said. 'The Championship Trophy would have meant a clean sweep.' It was not to be long however before Mick and his cohorts delivered that final coveted piece.

A Yorkshire Cup winner's medal was the only one missing from Roy Francis' collection, having come so close with Hull and Leeds, and having secured it, he opted to take up the challenge across the world in a groundbreaking full-time appointment which saw him given extensive power as North's manager-coach. John Atkinson analyses his legacy and overall influence on the club. 'Roy's departure was a bit disruptive. There was one night when we were training at Headingley just before he left when there were some Aussies watching us and we knew by the session that Roy was actually doing a PR job for himself. It lasted close on three hours and we went through every bit of our repertoire, and soon after we heard suggestions that he was going to North Sydney on a full-time basis. We were all, certainly the younger players anyway, absolutely devastated, but he was a conman; he used to lull you into doing things; we cottoned on very quickly but for us he was everything we wanted. He encouraged the backs in particular to play the rugby we wanted to play. It was the character of the team that got us through that period just after he went, we had some great players and eventually winning the Championship was the rebound from Roy. He had created something, a mindset in a lot of us where we knew we could do things and get ourselves in and out of trouble and that was a huge credit to him. It was everything that had been instilled; we knew we were fit enough and quick enough to get back and cover if things went wrong.

We had just achieved a blend of everything; Barry Seabourne had this fantastic tactical brain and deadly accurate kicking game, Mick was like having one-and-a-half players there on defence, Billy Ramsey was very domineering in the forwards, Syd Hynes was at his peak and probably the best centre in the world and he had this combination with Alan Smith that made you think they were telepathic, doing things to confuse the opposition, it was just instinctive. Tony Crosby used to say that he just ran up and down the centre of the pitch because he knew that eventually the ball would come to him if an outlet was needed in midfield. There were times when you might be having a bad time during a game and Mick was the one who was always there saying, "get up, come on, keep going, never mind, we're doing it", even if we were losing by 30 points. He had this long arcing run and you knew that eventually he would get to you and he'd want you for an offload or he'd go the other way to fool the defence – Johnny Whiteley used to say that it caused mayhem because he was a lot quicker than people assumed. Once he got into his stride he was so strong as we'd come from a generation where we'd done weight training all our lives, climbing trees and cross training, without knowing it. We were naturally fit and Roy built on that.'

By now Roy's protégées, with Barry Seabourne taking over as skipper, had an established repertoire with Hull Kingston Rovers and Huddersfield next on the receiving end of their attacking might as the Loiners ran in 62 points and twelve tries in four days. In their encounter with the Robins – who included legendary Aussie Arthur Beetson in their ranks – Mick took the Man of the Match award and along with Ray Batten, Alan Smith and John Atkinson celebrated his debut call-up for England, again initially as a substitute, for the forthcoming clash with the Welsh. Arthur Haddock's evocative description of the final touchdown epitomizes the way the side was playing. 'The sixth Leeds try in their sparkling 30-12 Headingley victory…was of such brilliance that the 6,000 crowd gave the players a standing ovation. It covered 90 yards, and with the ball being handled by Batten, Shoebottom (twice), Hynes, Albert Eyre and Seabourne, whose last pass sent Hick over. The breathtaking speed with which the players backed up and ran on to the ball put it among the best tries ever seen on this historic ground. This was yet another game in which Leeds turned on an astonishingly fast display that simply ran Rovers out of the park.' Mick was again designated as the star performer against Huddersfield when switching back to scrum-half, his distributive skills as much as his tearaway tackling confounding the Fartown outfit and resulting in another brilliant solo try. Such was his majestic form, another try accounting for York, that he gained his first domestic call-up for the Great Britain side scheduled to face France at St Helens at the end of November. The only consternation was that despite the club's tremendous run he was the only Loiner selected, leading to calls that the club had been deliberately snubbed. The revival of the England *v.* Wales fixture, after an absence of fifteen years, proved to be a double-edged sword for Mick. Played at Salford the day after the York match, he was drafted off the bench to start at scrum-half when Alex Murphy withdrew and aggravated his longstanding ankle problem in defeat. Despite intensive treatment he was forced out for three weeks which caused him to relinquish his GB spot although, ironically, he returned to the Leeds ranks at the same time as the televised Test, scoring another spectacular long-range try in an easy win over Bramley.

Roy Francis' protracted departure had seen dedicated, long-serving Alliance team coach Jack Nelson given the first team duties in a caretaker capacity, but tragedy struck when he died suddenly on Christmas Day, casting a pall over the club and the players as Bill Carter confirms. 'The players were hugely shaken by Jack's sudden death. He was very much a guiding force for Mick in his early days with the club, he had this ability to steady and direct his natural exuberance.' Billy Watts remembers it as a particularly difficult time which again needed the resolve and character of the players to pull the club through. 'Jack's death rocked the whole club. He was a lovely man, had been a good assistant coach under Roy and had brought so many of the youngsters, including Mick, through the ranks. He had a huge amount of respect from the players and all the coaching staff and it was a tragedy that he died so suddenly when he got his chance. The club was in a bit of turmoil at the time but the players just knitted together and became more determined and Mick, with his spirit, was a key part of that. He slotted in with them all, just dropped in with anybody socially and you always knew when he had arrived at the ground either for a match or training.' Alan Smith pays his own tribute. 'Jack Nelson's death was devastating, he was great for the "A" team, so many of the lads came through from it and that's why he was so proud to take over. He was a great loss.' Former coach, scout and administrator Joe Warham, who had managed the 1961 Championship-winning side, took over the reins in an emergency capacity. Varied training, which included taking his side for swimming sessions at the renowned International Pool in the city, kept the squad fresh, while on the work side Mick had changed jobs, moving from his old haunt at Bison's to become a steel frame maker for sign firm Oldham's. By the close of the calendar year he had amassed a total of 194 appearances for the Loiners; 144 of them at stand-off, 44 at scrum-half, 3 in the right centre and 3 from left centre accumulating 337 points from 83 tries and 44 goals.

Leeds extended their winning run throughout January which included a double over Featherstone, their captain, former Great Britain prop Mal Dixon, noting, 'their speed surprised us, they were yards faster than any other side we have played this season', as Mick took another Man of the Match award. The Challenge Cup defence began at Thrum Hall, Halifax, late in the month, the six-to-one favourites to retain their trophy just coming through a typically robust encounter before Mick turned his attention to the international stage and a trip to Toulouse for the return clash with the French after retaining his place in the Great Britain ranks. Again, though, it looked as though his selection would be ill-fated when he missed the bus to the airport and only just arrived in time to catch the plane and take his place alongside skipper Tommy Bishop. In the clash, which saw the hosts a much changed and improved outfit from the one which had gone down to heavy defeat at St Helens two months earlier, Shoey so nearly went from villain to hero. His uncharacteristi-cally suspect handling had gifted Francis de Nadai and Claude Matoulan tries as the French led 13-9 but six minutes from time it seemed like he would be given the chance to atone. John Mantle had put the game's costliest forward Colin Dixon clear and away and although Mick tore up in support on his inside frantically calling for what would have been the scoring – and match-winning pass – it never came, the Salford back-rower falling in the smother tackle of Jean Claude Clos. Mick, typically, took out his disappointment and evident frustration with a wonderful two-try performance to overwhelm Halifax at Headingley the following weekend on a snow-encrusted pitch. Hard-fought victory at Keighley in a twice postponed game saw Leeds through to the third round of the Challenge Cup and yet another away tie, this time at Castleford. It was a match that set the tone for the final encounter of the

The Great Britain line-up that lost at Toulouse in February 1969.

Awaiting the anthems, Mick second from the left with Colin Dixo next along.

campaign; the two sides literally slugging it out in front of over 13,000 fans who generated a threatening atmosphere and were warned on several occasions by referee Eric Lawrinson that he would call off the game if they persisted in throwing missiles, including bottles, onto the playing area. In an almost totally forward dominated battle, Shoey, and Barry Seabourne – who took a battering from the Castleford pack throughout and was eventually forced off injured – got little change out of Derek Edwards and Keith Hepworth, but Bev Risman's try edged the Loiners ahead just after the break. It looked like their staunch rearguard would hold but eight minutes from time Trevor Briggs crashed over to the delight of the home hordes and the holders were out, suffering their first defeat in sixteen games. Some consolation came by way of their retention of the Yorkshire League title as Leeds extended their unbeaten run in the Championship, although they had to settle for a draw in their first Sunday fixture at Hull. The match which secured that silverware was at Halifax a week later, again on a Sunday, with Mick the hero for an unstinting defensive effort in a side wracked by injuries. Over the Easter period Leeds met Batley twice in three days in totally contrasting encounters as they went after the League Leaders' crown for the third consecutive season. At Mount Pleasant Mick received his marching orders on the intervention of a touch judge just after the hour mark, following a flare-up after a scrum during which he claimed he was bitten. Seeking out referee Leach of St Helens after the game Shoey told him, 'I was in such pain that I had to clobber him to free myself'. Back at Headingley in the return game, and playing at scrum-half, his magnificent distribution set up an electrifying thirteen-try rout – including a brace for himself – and the biggest win of the season, 63-11. It prompted *Yorkshire Evening Post* reporter Leslie Temlett, in a homily to the Leeds style of play, to comment, 'Glorify? Yes. The word is not too strong; for it is very questionable whether any Leeds side has so delighted as this team of 1968/69...the Leeds of today has delighted as probably no other Leeds team has delighted in the past, because of its consistently brilliant teamwork. It has its stars, certainly. It is its teamwork, its co-ordination, that is its supreme asset...every man jack is to be congratulated, with special word for Mick Shoebottom, for that wonderful display of defensive work, interspersed with some of those sparkling thrusts for which he is renowned. A great show Mick! We all say "Thank you".'

A club record run of twenty-three successive Championship wins was ended on the final day of the regular season at Bradford as Leeds headed for the play-offs, the only concern for their fans a worry that they were susceptible to big packs keeping the ball tight and playing it up the middle. Mick, who had again received referee's warnings after a vendetta-ridden clash with Keighley, was out for the Odsal game and also missed the first round tie at home to Oldham, the disciplinary committee having shown little regard for his mitigating claims after the Batley biting incident and banning him for two matches. He was back for the play-off second round against Workington and was again called upon to set a defensive lead after the doughty Cumbrians had made the early running through their fearless forwards. He had already knocked-on with the line beckoning from Ray Batten's snap pass, had a drop goal attempt rebound off a post and been caught a yard out by a flying Paul Charlton before he scored the crucial try just after the half hour. John Atkinson broke the cover with a typical long striding burst and Mick darted inside to the posts to set up an 8-point lead which was the final victory margin. The semi-final against Salford, who were due at Wembley the following week, was an absolute thriller with the Loiners only edging clear in the final five minutes as their unbeaten home record was so nearly ended. They went into the game facing something of a forward crisis, Ken and Albert Eyre, David Hick and Peter Fozzard were out injured and with Joe Warham naming two backs on the bench out of necessity, the plan was to move Mick into the pack if there had been an injury to any of the forwards, 'a job' according to the caretaker coach, 'he was enthusiastically prepared to tackle'. The first half belonged to Colin Dixon whose two fine long-distance tries, when he showed a wonderful turn of pace, gave the Red Devils a 6-point lead at the break. Mick had vainly tracked him back on the second occasion. A Syd Hynes try straight after the re-start put the Loiners fans back in good heart but with Barry Seabourne constantly needing treatment for a four time dislocated shoulder it seemed that their creative edge was lacking. Only superb scrambling defence from Bev Risman kept Leeds in the game until Mick Clark, Ron Cowan and Syd Hynes broke in spectacular fashion to send hooker Tony Crosby over. Holding the narrowest of leads and under enormous pressure, late touchdowns to Ronnie Cowan and Ray Batten from Mick's instigation put the Loiners in their seventh Championship Final, eight years after their sole claiming of the blue ribbon prize.

ALAN HARDISTY HAS BEEN A MATCH WINNER IN THE PAST

BUT MICK SHOEBOTTOM WILL BE OUT TO SEE HE ISN'T ONE IN THE FUTURE

ODSAL STADIUM · BRADFORD

Rugby League Championship - Final

LEEDS

VERSUS

CASTLEFORD

SATURDAY 24th MAY 1969

KICK-OFF ~~2·0 p.m.~~ 3-15 p.m.

GRANDSTAND SECTION B

ROW **I**   SEAT NO.   **26**

20/-

G. W. Turton, Secretary

Opposite: Speed previews the Championship Final against Castleford.

Right: Ticket stub for the Championship Final, 1969.

There was a major scare in the blue and amber camp in the run up to the big decider, a fifth meeting of the season with arch rivals and Challenge Cup winners Castleford who were going for the double. Having complained about double vision in the days after the Salford match following a heavy knock on the head, Mick was diagnosed with delayed concussion and spent three days in hospital while his condition was closely monitored. The Leeds staff managed to keep his admission secret and it was only when he was released with full medical clearance that Joe Warham was able to announce the side that he hoped would make history. Imposing Ken Eyre was back at prop and Barry Seabourne's shoulder was deemed strong enough to lead his troops into battle, an ensemble desperate to crown their three-year reign as league leaders with the ultimate prize.

With so much at stake at a rain soaked Odsal and a turbulent series of matches already behind the protagonists that season, the Final is remembered as being one of the most brutal on record, with the early stages in particular littered by late challenges. As *Yorkshire Post* doyen Alfred Drewery put it, '…the virtues of courage and ability to soak up punishment were far more important than football skill'. Castleford lost their chief playmaker Malcolm Reilly after one high tackle too many and he failed to reappear for the second half along with Seabourne, whose shoulder had finally given way, and Mick Clark who suffered a nasty gash to the side of his head. By then Castleford led 11-7; Bev Risman having given Leeds an early advantage from a penalty after Keith Hepworth had been deemed guilty of feeding the first scrum only for Alan Hardisty to equalize with a coolly taken drop goal. Seabourne tried to answer in kind and when Hardisty charged down his effort, the ball spun through to Syd Hynes who sent Ronnie Cowan in at the corner. Within a couple of minutes the Glassblowers were back in front, hooker Clive Dickinson fooling a posse of Leeds defenders with his ball-juggling skills near the Leeds line, Tony Crosby's tackle from behind proving to be the impetus that drove him over the whitewash for the touchdown. Mick Redfearn converted and added a penalty soon after, Seabourne's long-range drop goal attempt bouncing off a post in reply before Ray Batten and Clive Dickinson were the next pair to come to blows. A foul on Castleford winger Tony Thomas saw referee Billy Thompson warn both captains, a third Redfearn penalty being cancelled out by one to Risman soon after. His skipper's absence meant that Mick moved to scrum-half after the break and his constant involvement became a key feature. Risman's third penalty narrowed the gap to 2 points as the vitriol on the field momentarily spilt onto the terraces, Hardisty intercepting in trademark fashion from Mick Joyce's clearing pass to gallop to the corner from 40 yards out, Risman's shepherd to keep him near the flag proving crucial as Redfearn pulled the conversion attempt wide.

At 14-9 down, the Loiners were in need of a moment of magic to regain the impetus and Mick provided it. Taking Bernard Watson's sweet reverse pass near his own line, Shoey saw a glimmer of a gap and was gone, haring towards glory only for Castleford full-back Derek Edwards to bring him down short. From the resulting play-the-ball, Ramsey dropped a goal to make the margin 3 points. Despite Leeds enjoying the best of the possession, two breaks from Thomas nearly took the trophy to Wheldon Road, Redfearn missing a penalty from the first and Cowan pulling off a try-saving tackle to halt the second. Five minutes from time the spoils were settled in glorious fashion which rewarded Leeds' indomitable spirit. A spiralling kick from Redfearn capriciously bounced over the heads of his chasers allowing Mick and Ken Eyre to scramble the ball clear to Risman on his own 25-yard line. A sprint to beat Dennis Hartley, a shimmy to deceive Trevor Briggs and he was away to near half way where his punt of unerring accuracy sat up deliciously for John Atkinson to race clear and over for a try near the posts that drew the teams level. There is a quintessential picture of Mick after that vital touchdown. With the other Leeds players trudging back, hands on hips, after congratulating the scorer, he is seen sitting alone near the half-way line centre field working out the score tally on his fingers, his total involvement such that he had no idea of the state of play. Atkinson thinks that the image sums up the man. 'The Championship Final was a bit hard! After I'd scored Mick was trying to work out how many points we needed to win. We'd got this intense rivalry and traditional resentment between the sides; we were two teams on top of their form although contrasting in styles. Castleford had massive forwards and great half-backs and we had a pack built by Roy that would do a job and allow the backs to do the rest. There were things going on throughout the game that had little place on a rugby field, it was as if the forwards didn't need the ball for a while, they were going to sort it all out before they started concentrating on rugby and yet there was some magic stuff played in between it all. As soon as you were tackled and were on the floor, you protected yourself, it was the accumulation of everything that had gone on between the rival sides that season. It worked out right for us and the exhaustion disappeared on the lap of honour, it kicked in again in the bath afterwards, you're on such a high because you've won and the realization of what it meant for the club. For a lot of us it was the satisfaction of knowing that we'd achieved and finally proved we were the best. We showed that not only could we play but we could successfully mix it with the best of them. A lot of people thought that

In the euphoria of John Atkinson's late equalizing try in the 1969 Championship Final at Odsal, Mick takes time out to add up the score.

Castleford would knock us off our game altogether but we refused to be intimidated. It was just a battle royal.'

Bev Risman's side-footed conversion ensured the coveted trophy was going to Headingley and he became the recipient of the Harry Sunderland Award, though for Eddie Waring, 'My vote cast before Risman's vital kick went to Hardisty and Shoebottom would have been my Leeds candidate for his versatile display.' That was not the end of the drama; as the game moved into injury time Mick again strode clear up the middle only for Dennis Hartley to flatten him and receive his marching orders. Harry Jepson looks back on that incident as summing up the no-quarter encounter. 'Mick relished that Championship Final; he loved it when it got physical; that was his type of match. Despite that it was a hell of a game and how Leeds pulled it out of the fire I'll never know. He was good friends with Dennis Hartley although that day Dennis was going round, right from the first scrum when he tried to take out Bill Ramsey, telling everyone how there were going to be no mates that afternoon.'

On the whistle there were scenes of unbridled joy amongst the Leeds players, Mick skipping and dancing in the style of Nobby Stiles as he paraded the trophy, along with Risman, on a jubilant lap of honour. Barry Seabourne sums up what that victory meant. 'Mick did a tremendous job moving to scrum-half after my shoulder came out again and finally locked. Derek Turner's instruction to the Castleford side was "to give us some pain" because he knew that we were quicker all round and Mick Clark and Shoey suffered because of that, but the victory meant more to us than Wembley, it was the culmination of everything we had been working for.' Alan Smith is in total agreement. 'Castleford were becoming a dominant team and when Malcolm left the field it made a real impact. They had some fantastic forwards but I've always found it strange and disappointing that the Leeds pack was often being questioned – and Derek Turner was one of the guys who frequently did. It was nice to get one over them in the Championship Final if only for that.'

A late break in a brutal decider, Dennis Hartley closes in on Shoey in an incident that was to see the Castleford prop dismissed.

Mick joyously parades the Championship Trophy with match-winning full-back Bev Risman.

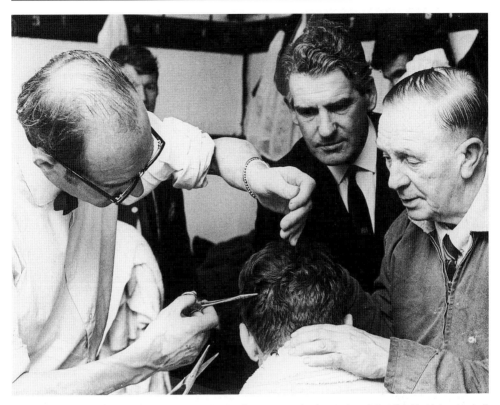

One of the toughest games ever seen. Dr Novis frantically tries to stitch a four-inch gash in Mick Clark's head at half time during the 1969 Championship Final as coach Joe Warham and kit man Arthur crowther show their concern.

Leeds Rugby League team shot 1968/69. From left to right, back row: Langley, Batten, Crosby, Clark, A. Eyre, Ramsey, Hick, K. Eyre, Atkinson. Front row: Smith, Hynes, Watson, Mr Warham, Seabourne, Mr Myerscough, Risman, Cowan, Shoebottom.

Although the turn out by the general public of the city was disappointing, the Leeds players celebrate their 1969 Championship success on the steps of the Civic Hall.

There was ecstasy amongst the players on the steps of the Civic Hall that evening as the team showed off the four trophies they had won in a glorious season, whilst attending a reception held in their honour by Lord Mayor Alderman Bretherick. Bev Risman sums up the mood. 'It meant everything, it was the pinnacle especially after getting to Wembley the year before, which had been a major goal for that side, and winning the League Leaders' so often but we'd never really finished it off with the title. That was a game when the big men really stood up and Mick absolutely revelled in it. When players did try and rough him up, even when he had the ball, he got the better of them and was looking for them out the other side of the collision. The big thing was he never took a backward step. The celebrations are a blur but we all went out together and although the Civic Reception was poorly attended, it meant more to us than the public, they'd seen us finish top of the League and the Championship Final in those days didn't have the same feeling the Super League Grand Final does now, it was just the icing on the cake. But to the club and the players it was everything.' The only disappointment was the scandalously low turnout that greeted them to acclaim their achievement, a paltry 400 or so fans milling about in the square and only a handful lining the three mile route from Headingley that their open-top bus took. Extra police had been drafted in to man crash barriers expecting similar hordes to those which had greeted Leeds United when they paraded their Championship a few days earlier, but they were stood down, prompting Seabourne to comment at the time, 'We felt like a right set of fools in that coach. I was very disappointed. You would have thought a team which had achieved what we have done would have had a better reception.' For Castleford, though, the desolation of defeat was made even greater when they heard that their coach, legendary hard man Derek 'Rocky' Turner, was leaving 'the Lane', having been lured up the road to their bitterest big city rivals.

8

1969/70
ON TOP OF THE WORLD

If ever a coach and a player were destined to get on it was Mick and Derek Turner. Two of the fiercest competitors in the toughest of sports, the Loiners' new coach recognized that he had a perfect, unyielding general on the field to do his bidding. As official timekeeper and key member of the behind-the-scenes support staff, Billy Watts recalls the respect between the pair. 'They were so similar as characters. Derek always used to say that when he selected his teams one name went down first of all and that was Mick's because he could move him to wherever he needed him. He knew that no matter where he put Mick, either at the start or during the game, he would get eighty minutes out of him.' Shoey responded by playing the best and most consistent rugby of his career in a season which would culminate in the selection of the fourteenth Lions tourists. He was further heartened by two pieces of good news at the start of the campaign; Leeds opting not to sign Aussie Test stand-off Dennis Pittard on a short-term contract and one of his main rivals for a Great Britain spot, Tommy Bishop, deciding to emigrate to Sydney to invigorate fledgling club Cronulla-Sutherland. Pittard's pedigree was obvious, the current Rothmans Medal holder for his supreme displays with a dominant South Sydney – he was later to become one of a very select band to win the honour twice – he had just made his debut for the Kangaroos on their tour to New Zealand. Despite his obvious potential commercial value to the club with likely increased gates at a time when the code was struggling, the Leeds management decided against disrupting their star-studded back line or risk potential upset to the squad's obvious close camaraderie and morale.

With Barry Seabourne still recovering from an inevitable shoulder operation, Mick went into battle predominantly in the number seven shirt for the opening couple of months, clearly relishing being at the epicentre of the action and forming a devastating combination with loose forward Ray Batten, as club Secretary Bill Carter remembers. 'He built up a wonderful understanding with Ray and fed off him in the middle of the field. I know Michael was very appreciative of Ray's handling skills.' Alan Smith, who was on the end of so much of their spadework, was another massive admirer. 'Ray had such dexterity around the pack but when you say Shoey was determined and enthusiastic it tends to hint that those qualities made up for a lack of skill but it didn't, he was always scheming. Barry Seabourne had the silky little

Shoey in full flight against Huddersfield on 27 September 1969.

passes and was a fantastic tactical kicker and Shoey loved to patrol the middle defensively, it was a great combination.'

Two totally contrasting ties opened Leeds' defence of the Yorkshire Cup. Against Bradford at Headingley, referee Joe Manley's leniency saw the contest degenerate into a bitter battle with rugby occasionally breaking out amongst the incessant altercations. Mick's early touchdown set the holders on their way but equally as important was his sensational one-on-one tackle to push Geoff Clarkson back from between the posts when seemingly a certain scorer. It was an incident that Batten recalls with a smile. 'I remember Geoff Clarkson coming through on the charge and despite weighing two-and-a-half stone less, Mick picked him up by the knees and drove him back 5 yards or so before dumping him – that summed him up.' Halifax were simply blitzed in the second round, Trevor Watson in the *Yorkshire Evening Post* calling the eight-try display 'dazzling', adding, 'the Headingley backs…sparkled, Shoebottom looking sharper than for some seasons. Some of his breaks came out of nothing.' Leeds' passage to the Final seemed assured when they led 17-11 at Hull going into the final stages, but a 10-point rally by the Airlie Birds to snatch victory was a real blow. Derek Turner called his side in for extra training after that display along with unconvincing wins over Wakefield and York which saw another second half fade out. The only constant seemed to be Mick, who was Man of the Match against the Minstermen, 'He was the difference, he had more drive than any other player' said Arthur Haddock, whilst the following week against Hunslet Alfred Drewry commented in the *Yorkshire Post:* 'If Shoebottom had not strayed football wise from the side of the river he was brought up and still lives, Hunslet would probably have won.' That match seemed to encapsulate everything Mick was about on the field. He earned the wrath of the Parkside fans when he was cautioned for a foul on eighteen-year-old centre Stephen Hudson as he put the home side ahead, but before the booing had died down his tremendous run down the left flank paved the way for Ken Eyre to level. With the match in the balance, home winger Tommy Thompson was put clear and away only for Shoey to find 'phenomenal reserves of speed to cut him off with a flying tackle right at the corner' which turned the game. In the sixty-fifth minute, with the Loiners holding onto a 10-5 lead, he delivered the coup de grace with a remarkable solo touchdown. Receiving a pass, he stopped, took a good look around which seemed to mesmerize the defenders before showing astonishing acceleration, this time from a standing start to waltz past six of them to the line. Before the next game at home to Bradford, the supporters' club notes in the match programme noted, 'What a good job we have Shoey. Out of touch as we are, he's the one shining star. If there's a better half-back around we've not seen him this season. And not likely to if he keeps this form up.'

The reintroduction of an official European Championship after an absence of thirteen years saw Mick called up to the England squad for the first batch of fixtures against the Welsh at Headingley, which he missed out on, and France a week later at Wigan, although he was selected on the bench as Roger Millward and captain Alex Murphy took the starting half back spots. It prompted the first of a series of debates about likely tour candidates although Derek Turner, himself a Lion in 1962 when with Wakefield, was in no doubt. 'You have got to have hungry players and real professionals to do the job over there, like Mick Shoebottom and Bev Risman. Mick isn't as classy as Bev but he's a real pro. When you get out to Australia everybody has to want to play. There's a job to be done and you've got to get down to it. You have to have men like Shoebottom', he told Jack Bentley of the *Daily Express.* There was a measure of compensation when Leeds became the inaugural European Club Champions as Perpignan were downed 31-5 at Headingley, in a match convened to promote the advent of colour television although, somewhat ironically, four days later they were bundled out of the BBC Floodlit Competition at Castleford. As so often, Mick responded to such adversity with redoubled efforts and hit a purple patch during December as Leeds consolidated their place at the top of the table, carrying off four consecutive Man of the Match awards. He grabbed two and created most of the other six tries as Dewsbury were humbled before inspiring a late rally to overcome Bradford at Odsal in his 250th appearance in blue and amber. It was another run of form that underlined his value to John Atkinson, appreciating his skills from out on the flank. 'Mick played rugby as if he was Derek's psyche. 'Rocky' built from the pack outwards and although he eventually got the sack because of the style of rugby we were playing, I scored more tries under him than any other coach. He didn't want Mick to do as much tackling because he knew he was such an attacking weapon, but you couldn't stop him from just wanting to be totally involved. It was like winding him up and just sending him out there for eighty minutes. When he hit someone properly in the tackle, you could see the beaming smile on his face.' Headingley's under-soil heating ensured the clash with championship rivals Featherstone went ahead, Barry Wood leading his match report with,

'I've said it before and say it again, Mick Shoebottom, Leeds' fiery Test star, is the best all-round stand-off in the game. On a day when the champions struggled to hit top form Shoebottom, running and tackling with tremendous pace and power, did more than anyone to extend Leeds' unbeaten home League run to thirty-seven games.' Fred Trueman's analysis in his Sunday column was, 'The only man to reach any great heights was Shoebottom. A proper slippery eel Rovers just couldn't get a firm grip on him.' On Boxing Day, revenge was sweet against Castleford, Mick scoring the first try, setting up the clincher for David Hick and outplaying tour rival Alan Hardisty as Leeds triumphed 8-0 in front of just under 19,000 captivated fans, the code's biggest crowd of the season.

Again, after such imperious form, the International Selectors were forced to look at his claims for the Ashes tour as the season reached its halfway point at the calendar year end. In leading articles, speculation was rife but it was clear that Mick had his fans. Ramon Joyce, analysing the claims of all the candidates, wrote '…he is playing better than ever now. He has lost a few pounds but none of his power and looks a little bit faster. Shoebottom is regarded by many as one of the tour "certs" but he will be the last to be optimistic. Despite his consistency, he has played only twice for Great Britain (not including substitute appearances) – once as a centre in the World Cup. He was in England's squad for the international series in October, but made only a brief appearance as a substitute full-back.' With tobacco brand Players No.6 offering a total of £600 prize money for the leading recipients of Man of the Match awards and four of the leading seven names being stand-offs – Mick's eight nominations seeing him in joint fourth place – the competition was clearly intense. Arthur Haddock solicited the opinion of four of the leading coaches and former Lions stars and all of them; John Whiteley, Ken Traill, Tommy Harris and Eric Ashton, included Mick as one of their two choices. Again Haddock pointed to Mick's loss of weight as the a key factor behind his eye-catching displays. 'Shoebottom tells me the reason is that he was a bit too heavy starting the season at 13st 3lb and has reduced to 12st 6lb, his best weight. He came home from the 1968 World Cup series in Australia weighing 13st 10lb' Mick freely admitted that his dogged will to shed the pounds and devotion to training had been partly driven by the reaction of his team-mates. 'Some of the Leeds boys laughed at me', he said, 'but I was determined to trim myself down to my best weight. It was hard going at times but I did it. Now it means I can find that all-important extra yard of pace.'

His excellent reviving try to set up a significant win at Wigan was rewarded with the squad being taken to Blackpool to prepare for the forthcoming Challenge Cup, which Chairman Jack Myerscough confidently believed Leeds could regain. 'I would like to get to Wembley', he opined. 'I think it can be said that we can look forward to the second half of the season, knowing that we have a fair chance in all that is going. Nobody could ask for more. They are a grand, happy family. The spirit is tremendous and there is no doubt it will remain so.' Lowly Batley gave the Loiners, 7-2 favourites for the cherished silverware, a torrid time at Headingley before finally succumbing in the opening round. A week later, with preparations hampered by bad weather which saw training switched indoors under the South Stand, Leeds travelled to face Warrington on a Wilderspool quagmire. Mick's early try near the posts after a great run by Bev Risman set up a titanic struggle with the visitors holding a slender 8-5 lead at the break. The score stayed like that until injury time as both sides strove desperately for the crucial score in the pouring rain, it coming at the death when Barry Seabourne's

Mick tops the show again

Leeds 8
Castleford 0   ★★★★

MICK SHOEBOTTOM out-played talented rival Alan Hardisty, the Castleford skipper, in Headingley thriller.

He collected the man-of-the-match honours for the fourth time running. For good measure Shoebottom got Leeds on the right track to a revenge win by snapping the first try and then spirited off the match-clinching try by David Hick near the end.

Leeds made it 38 league wins in a row at home on merit, but as usual lively Castleford took them all the way.

If Castleford had been able to crown spirited approach work in the proper way they could easily have gained their third victory over Leeds this season.

They had more of the attacking play with forwards Brian Lockwood and Mick Redfearn leading the way but were short of finishing punch in the middle.

Lock was unlucky in the opening quarter when he put the ball over the bar but the referee ruled that he had punted the ball and the 'goal' did not count.

Castleford went near a try twice through Alan Lowndes and Trevor Briggs but they could not pierce a resolute Leeds defence in which Bill Ramsey and Ray Batten starred.

Mike Shoebottom dives over for the vital Leeds try

Shoebottom 'hat-trick' boost for Tourists

From BRIAN BATTY, TOWNSVILLE, Queensland

MIKE SHOEBOTTOM, Britain's stand off, scored a hat-trick of tries, just missed a fourth, and then went off injured as the tourists hung on to beat North Queensland 23pts. to 20 here yesterday.

The brilliant Leeds international proved a handful for the rugged Australians, especially in the opening stages when Britain looked set for a runaway win.

Shoebottom was taken off in the last minute of the match suffering from a thigh injury, but it is not serious.

North Queensland 20pts.,
Great Britain 23

The tourists appeared to lose their drive towards the end with the heat sapping their energy. They also looked unsettled, conceding 19 penalties in the match, but even so the overall signs were most encouraging.

In addition to Shoebottom's efforts, Britain's other scores were tries by Lowe and Laughton, and four goals by Dutton.

Star of the Australian side was Harold Menadu, their bearded Aborigine full-back, who kicked seven goals.

He was responsible for Queens-

land's second-half surge, which saw them hit back from 23—8 to 23—20 in a desperate bid for victory.

Shoebottom's penalty try soon after the interval proved to be the deciding score.

He dribbled the ball over the line, but was prevented from following it up and a resultant penalty try gave Britain a 21—8 lead, increased to 23—8 when Dutton landed the goal.

Britain look the winning handsomely when they set off at a great rate in the first half.

They led 11—0 after 15 minutes and 16—2 after half-an-hour's play. But they gave away too many penalties—they had 19 awarded against them in the match compared with seven against North Queensland—and later in the game their tackling lapsed.

The game became over-robust late in the first half. Laughton and Hartley were both cautioned twice and Hynes and Robinson once each.

—Aussies must keep an eye on Shoebottom

By DEREK MARSHALL

IF Mick Shoebottom can maintain his present form he should be a sensation in Australia.

Currently, neither of his two talented tour rivals can match him in all-round ability.

The Leeds stand-off half may be a trifle slower than Hardisty and Millward, but he is no less devastating. His work rate is higher than Hardisty's and his durability and strength greater than that of Millward.

Shoebottom, in fact, was the mainspring behind the 47—5 thrashing of Hull in the second semi-final.

There were no excuses for Rovers. The absence of Millward was a cruel blow but it simply could not explain the way they were out-thought, out-run, and out-manoeuvred at every turn.

There were some dazzling individual Leeds performances, notably from Hynes, Eccles, Ramsey, and Seabourne, while Atkinson rounded things off with a wing try reminiscent of the Bevan era.

'Shoebottom is a tour certainty'

Mick Shoebottom

Before the R.L. international selectors name 26 players for the tour of Australia and New Zealand, arguments will rage among supporters regarding the composition of the party.

One player who has already booked his passage "Down Under" is surely Leeds off-half Mick Shoebottom, whose dynamic drive has devastated opposing defences in many matches this season. His tenacious tackling and barnstorming bursts are the right attributes for a tourist.

However, although his selection appears a formality there are many rivals for the No. 6 berth. Leading contenders are Millward (Hull K.R.), Hardisty (Castleford), Brophy (Barrow), Morgan (Hunslet) Myler (St. Helens), and Watkins (Salford).

There is a shortage of outstanding threequarters, and consequently it would seem logical to nominate Shoebottom for centre, where he has previously played with distinction.

He could give additional cover for either of the half-back positions, which should be filled in the first place by Millward, Hardisty, Murphy and Seabourne.

S. PEPPER,

Roseville Terrace, Leeds.

Four-headline montage from 1970.

clever reverse pass sent Syd Hynes over and Leeds to Craven Park for a quarter-final tussle with Hull Kingston Rovers. Before that and three days after the heroic defeat of the Wire – and in a portent of what was to come – a quintet of Loiners backs were lining up for England in the reverse European Championship fixtures, first facing Wales at Headingley. The combination of Smith, Atkinson, Hynes, Shoebottom and Seabourne proved to be the difference with five of the six tries in a 26-7 win coming from the home-based contingent.

There was doubt about the eagerly awaited match with Hull Kingston Rovers right until the last minute, referee Joe Manley deciding just before the kick-off – as Leeds were arriving – that the mud bath pitch was playable. Forward dominance in such conditions was always going to be the key and in Phil Lowe, Cliff Wallis and Terry Clawson the hosts had a distinct advantage, former Leeds star Geoff Wrigglesworth claiming the only try in a 7-2 Rovers success which was more comprehensive than the scoreline suggested. For Mick there was solace in the announcement of twenty-one of the twenty-six names to go on tour, the selectors keeping five places open for form men in the closing weeks of the season. Along with his England colleagues, he was in; the first time that Leeds had five representatives in a Lions party. All of them travelled to Toulouse for the game against France and although disappointingly defeated 14-9, England took the European title on points difference. According to Alfred Drewry, 'Shoebottom, playing with his usual zest, was the only English back who impressed.'

Injury against Bramley forced Mick to miss the last five championship matches as Leeds retained the Yorkshire League title and collected the League Leaders' Trophy for an unprecedented fourth consecutive campaign, but he was back in style for the play-offs.

Five of the six Leeds players who represented England in the 1970 European Championships, from left to right: Bob Haigh, Mick Shoebottom, Alan Smith, John Atkinson and Syd Hynes.

The five Leeds players, all backs, selected for the 1970 Ashes Tour. From left to right, top row: Alan Smith, Syd Hynes. Seated: John Atkinson, Barry Seabourne and Mick Shoebottom.

Against Halifax he scored a spectacular touchdown causing Freddie Trueman to comment, 'The message to the Aussies from tour man Shoebottom is "watch out". He was so full of beans that he even took on the hefty members of the Halifax pack. His corking try…had the grandstand regulars on their feet in sheer admiration. He picked up at a play-the-ball on the Halifax 25 and got into his long stride straightaway to swerve past three defenders and leave them standing.' Whitehaven, who had shocked Wigan in the previous round, were next to be put to the sword in a thrilling Headingley exhibition which saw the Loiners run in eleven tries – one for every year since they had last played the Cumbrians – ten of them to the backs. Mesmerizing interplay thrilled the home crowd with Mick upstaging his effort against Halifax when he claimed a sensational opening score. Eddie Waring called him 'Mick the Knife' for carving open the visiting defence in the third minute; Arthur Haddock recounting that, 'a super solo effort beat at least half a dozen men for the try of the season. He twisted and turned, dummied and accelerated, and finally outpaced Donnelly to send the Leeds fans into a frenzy of delight as he sped over.' That was from 35 yards out, his second after the interval from double that distance. The semi-final brought the chance of revenge with Challenge Cup conquerors Hull Kingston Rovers the visitors, Shoey producing arguably his finest eighty minute stint in the famous colours. Described by Leslie Temlett as 'a human tornado', his hat-trick inside the opening twenty-six minutes – in stunning tandem with Syd

113

Hynes – had spectators and reporters drooling. Ian Cameron called it, 'spellbinding rugby from the Leeds wizards. The Headingley crowd basked in the limelight of a fantastic display of penetrating running and switched-on combination passing. Rovers…didn't have an answer. They suffered a body blow before the match when kingpin Millward cried off…but they would have needed thirteen superstars to have dammed the torrent of football and ideas which flowed from Leeds. Stand-off Shoebottom was the Crown Prince, scoring four brilliant tries and having a hand in everything that went on. His third try came after a fabulous inter-passing duet with Hynes which wouldn't have disgraced the circus ring. He and the centre handled the ball three times each in a touchline trail which had poor Rovers thoroughly bemused…Shoebottom careering across field and then changing direction to go in for a try which raised the roof.' Alfred Drewery pointed out, 'Never has a rout been more complete in an important match. Leeds scored more points than Goole (all out 35) scored runs in a Yorkshire Council cricket match on the other side of the stand.' For Bill Carter it was a seminal display. 'Mick always loved the big occasions and in that play-off semi-final he was really on fire. I saw him have a lot of wonderful matches for Leeds throughout the years but I think that one was his finest performance; it was a truly excellent, dazzling display that tore apart a very good side virtually single-handedly.' A sensational afternoon was literally crowned when Jack Myerscough presented the five upcoming Lions tourists and Ray Batten with their international caps.

With 116 points scored in three play-off ties, Leeds went into the decider with St Helens at Odsal a fortnight later as clear favourites to retain their Championship crown but, as so often in the tortuous history of the club, their form slipped at the defining moment. Like the changing weather, which threw thunder, lightning and hail at the protagonists after a glorious start, Leeds scored two early tries to hold a narrow half-time lead before falling away as the Saints forwards – with John Mantle and Cliff Watson stand outs – gradually got on top. What had always been perceived of as the Loiners' weakness had come back to haunt them when it really mattered. Mick's spirit and determination in the Final never wavered although he barely recovered from an early knock which hampered his effectiveness. For the *Yorkshire Evening Post*'s Arthur Haddock, 'It was a final containing much that is best in Rugby League. Leeds made such a good start…that it seemed as if this was going to be their day. About fifteen minutes after half-time the St Helens pack clearly began to get the upper hand in the loose and this, coupled with a fall-off by the Leeds inside backs (except the indefatigable Shoebottom), became the deciding factor.' Alan Smith was philosophical about the disappointment, 'Derek really threw it at us at half-time and said, "you five, who are going on tour, you've really got the blues" and he actually had a real go at us. Whether there was any psychology in that I don't know but Saints were a very good side and that's sport.' John Atkinson is equally phlegmatic about how what had looked like being an historic campaign had ended tinged in underachievement. 'I don't think we consciously raised our game during 1970 because we knew there was a tour on. A few of us had an idea that we must be in with a good chance because the back division was causing havoc throughout that season. Not retaining the Championship though was just Leeds. We were brilliant at times but because of the way we'd all been brought up to play when we came together, it wasn't unusual that we sometimes got beaten. We just didn't know how to close games down, it wasn't natural to us, and we'd often open up on our own line, drop the ball and lose the game. On balance I'm glad because it paid off more than it didn't.' Some personal recompense came with Mick being named the Leeds Supporters' Club Player of the Year by an overwhelming majority, an accolade that carried with it the eventual presentation of an electric blanket. It was an award that clearly meant a lot to him. 'We had a good bond with the fans, we always went down to the old Bowling Club which they used as the social club at Headingley after training in those days and the supporters just loved him, there was always a really close affinity', Alan Smith recounts.

Three days later a large crowd of friends and relatives were at Manchester airport to wave Jack Harding's men off on an arduous three month tour of the Antipodes. By then Mick had already contrived to miss the official photo call. Whilst in Blackpool on pressing business, he suddenly remembered that he should have been at Headingley, his subsequent late arrival being blamed on traffic problems. Word had already reached Australia about his form and prowess, with legendary hard man and pre-war Test prop Ray Stehr, later a respected commentator, a more than interested spectator when watching the Loiners' Headingley demolition of Hull Kingston Rovers in early May. Shoey left with the words of journalist Derek Marshall endorsing his representative claims. 'If Mick Shoebottom can maintain his present form', he noted, 'he should be a sensation in Australia. Currently, neither of his two talented tour rivals can match him in all round ability. The Leeds stand-off half may be a trifle slower than Hardisty and Millward, but he is no less devastating. His work rate is higher than Hardisty's and his durability and strength greater than that of Millward.' Similarly, Eddie Waring wrote in his feature column, 'Millward has been voted Player of the Year by the Player's No.6 judges, but for me the outstanding player has been Leeds stand-off Mick Shoebottom. Until this season I rated Shoebottom just a shade behind Hardisty and Millward, but his consistency, culminating in some fantastic displays in the play-offs, gets him my number one vote now.'

There was genuine optimism amongst the British players, staff and journalists that the departing squad was capable of regaining the Ashes, narrowly surrendered in controversial circumstances in 1966. A relatively young but internationally experienced party was dubbed as one of the best to leave these shores with all twenty-six players easily capable of and eventually actually stepping up to Test match level during the time away under the wily stewardship of hugely respected captain Frank Myler and coach Johnny Whiteley. A thirty-six-hour flight to Darwin followed by barely eighteen hours' rest and acclimatization was hardly ideal preparation for the most exacting of schedules, the Lions facing five matches in nine days leading up to the first Test in Brisbane. Mick sat out the opening clash against a young and inexperienced Northern Territories side that seemed determined to make a name for themselves by, almost literally at times, taking the scalp of their illustrious guests. He made his bow two days later at Townsville, scene of his 1968 triumph, and again grabbed the headlines with a sparkling display which yielded a hat-trick of touchdowns – including a game-breaking penalty try at the start of the second half – and saw him just miss a fourth in a narrow 23-20 victory over Barry Muir's North Queensland. His speedy darts were a constant menace, Brian Batty reported, 'The brilliant Leeds international proved a handful for the rugged Australians, especially in the opening stages when Britain looked set for a runaway win.' This put Mick firmly in the frame for a place in the First Test line-up although troublesome thigh and buttock injuries, partly sustained by grass burns from the baked surface, saw him substituted late on.

The 1970 Lions squad set out on their historic Ashes tour.

Media opinion in Australia was divided about the strength of the touring party, some claiming even at this early stage that they looked capable of providing the sternest of opponents for their old foes while respected *Sydney Daily Mirror* correspondent Bill Mordey warned the Lions about their tactics. He told them that they could expect 'savage retaliation from some Australian "bad guys" which could turn the series into a bloodbath if they persisted in "head-hunting" and refused to tackle low.' Certainly Doug Laughton and Dennis Hartley twice, and Syd Hynes and Dave Robinson had all received cautions in the Townsville heat. Mordey claimed that Aussie Manager Bill Robinson had told him after the North Queensland game that, 'They may be able to get away with rough tactics against inexperienced sides, but the stronger teams they'll meet in the coming weeks won't put up with it.' It was a prophecy that was borne out by the three match series, however Mordey's assertion that the tourists' defence looked suspect ultimately came back to haunt him.

Of more concern to the Great Britain management was the high penalty count against their sides, 38-11, after the opening two encounters with most offences for being offside or in the scrum. Mick sat out a third victory over Central Queensland at Rockhampton, the graze and lump on his leg causing a swelling in his groin which necessitated an unconventional solution for his next appearance against Wide Bay at peanut-growing and dairy town Wondai. Taking the advice of star Aussie centre Reg Gasnier and following in the footsteps of the 1958 tourists, he donned women's nylon panties under his shorts, saying, 'I'll cut the frills off the legs and these should be just the job.' As Alan Smith recalls, what others may have thought of the idea never entered Mick's head. 'It just didn't bother him one bit. He said "give 'em here" and proudly displayed them to all and sundry as he pranced around the dressing room in them.' It led to him gaining a notorious nickname from some of his team-mates for the remainder of the tour as his brother George relates. 'He was immensely proud of playing in Australia; he always said that it was a fabulous experience. In one match he had his shorts ripped and he had these knickers on underneath. After that all his team-mates used to shout "here comes the lady", but that was typical Mick, he was so placid off the field and used to let everyone take the Mickey out of him but as soon as he put a jersey on that was it.' The unconventional attire did the trick and Mick crossed for a try in a 45-7 romp which saw all of the Leeds contingent post touchdowns. Rated as the best British back in the first half, the Lions played some superb flowing rugby until the heat and the hosts' use of six substitutions – which tour manager Jack Harding described as farcical - sapped their energy.

By now a routine was starting to develop, as Barry Seabourne relates. 'We used to change round the rooming arrangements, but one rule Johnny Whiteley had was that club mates should not share so as to avoid cliques. We went to a lot of functions together as a team but there wasn't a lot of time to socialize because the schedule was so heavy.' John Atkinson gives additional insight. 'We left England not knowing how well everyone was going to get on. I'd always been close with Clive Sullivan and we roomed together which was brilliant because he'd been a paratrooper and he could get up early and make toast and press your trousers. All the lads within a very short time came together. There's always a feeling amongst you at the start where you look round and think, "should he be here, is he really good enough to be with us?" and a lot of us were surprised Billy Benyon wasn't selected. In the end only Barry Seabourne and Derek Edwards were really homesick and they used to go to the pictures together all the time. We had it quite easy from Darwin down to Brisbane – apart from the country sides trying to knock our heads off – and everybody started pulling as one. The Leeds five only ever played together once and the night before the game four of us roomed together – it was the only time that I had jetlag and couldn't sleep a wink. Mick was the life and soul, if there was any mischief or wind of a party he was at the centre of it. It didn't take long for the lads who didn't know him on tour to realize that this bloke was a bit special.'

Rested again for the comprehensive defeat of Queensland in Brisbane a week before the opening international there, in which significantly half-back pairing Roger Millward and Keith Hepworth were outstanding, there was widespread surprise when Mick was included in the unfamiliar role of centre in place of club mate Syd Hynes for the First Test. Rather than wanting to break the tried and tested Castleford combination of Alan Hardisty and Keith Hepworth in midfield but feeling the need for Shoey's defensive solidity and drive, the selectors partnered him with skipper Frank Myler in the three-quarters. Preparations were not helped when up-and-coming youngster Malcolm Reilly was served a writ after an alleged head-butting incident at a midweek private party which nearly forced the tour management to send him home. Only the intercession of a delegation of players who claimed he had been deliberately targeted and the collective paying of his fines and subsequent court costs saved his place. It was symptomatic of the kind of bonds that were being created, as Alan Smith recalls with obvious fondness. 'The Ashes tour was the highlight, it was one big high, and we were just young, fit lads raring to go – especially Shoey. If you were a utility man you were often seen as a sub but ask anyone around that time, you put Mick in and then built the team around him. There couldn't have been a better tourist because of his dressing room banter and his jovial, almost roguish, attitude, he was a coach's dream with his boundless enthusiasm in the dressing room, on the field or socially. He was a social animal, he was the first up for going out, if anybody had any thoughts of homesickness, he was the man who banished them. For me going to Leeds from nar Wakefield used to be a long way but finding myself in Aussie, the first twenty-four hours seemed strange and I wondered what I was doing there, it was the same for Barry Seabourne and Derek Edwards, but Shoey was the first to get you out of any idea of feeling miserable. He teamed up with "Flash" Flanagan who was always the first to get up and sing, and who was going to be the first to be the clown? – Shoey.'

'My one abiding memory of him on that tour was when we were in the Railway Hotel in Brisbane. If the lads today could see the sort of place it was they wouldn't believe it, it was the worst hotel I have ever stayed in – the Olympic in Sydney was posh by comparison, despite the lady with the lipstick and the thumb in your soup. The Railway was something else, it had painted floor-boards and like a white toilet downstairs which was the bar. We all dragged the jukebox upstairs to create some atmosphere; it was part of the bonding process living together in such squalor for two weeks. Mick and "Flash" had retired early because they were playing the next day and I was sitting in one of the rooms with a few of the guys who weren't selected for that game writing a letter home when I looked up and a rat came through the door from the top of the landing. It shot between my legs and then doubled back. There was an old settee in the room which, if you hit it, clouds of dust came up and drifted across like a scene from the desert, and Dennis Hartley, Roger Millward and Malcolm Reilly were lounging on it. I jumped up and kicked this rat and it rolled under the settee where the lads were sitting. They leapt off and one of them lifted it up, and as this rat ran out for the door Malcolm swung his leg at it, caught it full on and it went splat, squashed flat on the opposite wall. There was only one thing to do with it when we realized who was in bed so Malcolm went and banged on the door and shouted to Shoey, getting the response, "What? Go away!" Knock, knock, knock again, "Flash, here, couple of birds to see you". "(Expletive) sod off!" By now we'd got them to the other side of the bedroom door with any excuse that was some sort of a party going on. In Brisbane all the doors have got fan lights for ventilation above them and Malcolm lobbed in this dead rat and you should have heard the screams from the two of them. I'd love to have seen their faces as they jumped into bed hugging one another. Mick gave us some stick from in the room and the next morning when he came out but there was never any nastiness, he was still the same jolly fellow able to see the funny side.' John Atkinson was another of those present at the time. '"Flash" came through the door without opening it, he was frightened to death of being on his own or being in the dark on his own and he always used to room with Shoey, they were a bit of a comedy double act. I think "Flash" fell in love with Mick, he couldn't believe he'd got this even larger-than-life figure alongside him.'

The Lions went into the First Test as clear favourites with most pundits predicting a likely win in front of a sellout crowd of nearly 43,000 at Lang Park. What still worried GB manager Jack Harding and coach Johnny Whiteley most was the high penalty count against their side, especially with supreme kicker Graeme Langlands in the Aussie ranks and captaining them from full-back for the first time. Mick opposed debutant John Brass a former Wallaby who had turned professional with Eastern Suburbs two years earlier and was one of three newcomers in the home ranks. Another of them, prop Jim Morgan, was to play the key role in a massive upset, his two tries setting up a conclusive 37-15 success, as did his part in a huge melee which saw British prop Cliff Watson sent off just after half-time after shattering Morgan's nose. That was one of a number of unsavoury incidents as the complacent Lions pack lost their composure in the face of a constant barrage from Morgan and Arthur Beetson; Langlands kicking nine goals from eleven attempts as penalties abounded following a series of high shots. Sacrificing rugby for robustness, the tourists quickly learnt a valuable lesson, although the Aussie injury toll – Ron Lynch suffering a depressed fracture of the cheekbone, Beetson and Langlands broken noses and Phil Hawthorne leg injuries – reduced their effectiveness and made them extremely wary for the remainder of the series. A contemplative Whiteley wistfully identified the flaws in his side's tactics: 'We never moved into tackles. We never made our passes stick. And we never really hurt them', he said. Mick's influence was limited in such forward dominated exchanges. The *Sydney Morning Herald* noted, 'There were rare occasions when Britain's centres Mick Shoebottom and Frank Myler looked dangerous, but generally they were well covered and forced across field by the straight line of Australia's defence.' While *Rugby League Week*, as part of a scathing article deriding the side as 'innocuous, pitiful and leaving a sick taste in the mouth', rated Mick as 'nothing in attack. Made a few orthodox tackles but not sharp enough with the ball.' John Atkinson is convinced that compromise cost the side that Test but it also provided an invaluable lesson.

Mick is hauled down during the First Test in Brisbane.

'Mick played centre to me at Lang Park and we got walloped, it was a bad selection. We didn't play well, we all struggled that day but I think Johnny Whiteley was the first to agree that we made some selection errors. It didn't really matter to Mick where he was picked because he just wanted to enjoy himself out on the field, he thought it was wonderful. That defeat really brought us together and another factor was that Johnny had been on the 1958 tour which held the record for most wins and once we started to creep towards it that became a goal for the squad. He used to say "You'll never do it", and we'd reply "We bloody will" and that bonded the guys together to become really good friends. We'd spent so long knocking seven bells out of each other domestically but we just became this massive unit.'

There was little time for the British players to respond to the vitriol as the day after the Test debacle they were back in action at Toowoomba. Mick reverted to scrum-half and in a typically effective display scored a try in a comfortable 37-13 success with Syd Hynes claiming a hat-trick and Alan Smith also crossing. Before they left Queensland, there was another incident that increased the camaraderie of the Lions, as Alan Smith recalls. 'It was after defeat in the First Test that it really started to gel together so well. There was also the incident involving Malcolm. We were on the plane in Brisbane taxiing to take off for the next leg of the tour in Sydney when this car came onto the tarmac and obviously radioed to the pilot to stop the plane. It slowed down and we knew there had been this problem with Malcolm and that the authorities were likely to be coming after him. Two men came on board, both solicitors, and they went into the cockpit. After a short while the pilot came on the intercom and said, "We need to speak to one of the members of the Great Britain touring party before we can take off, would a mister Malcolm Reilly please press his overhead steward's button to make himself known." Twenty-eighty hands went up instantly and simultaneously, players and staff, and they weren't able to serve their writ. They caught up with him eventually but it just showed the togetherness and spirit we all had.' In Sydney, back at the infamous Olympic Hotel, the mounting criticism of the Lions intensified when television allegations called the tourists 'a beer swilling, pot-bellied lot who don't train', which served only to bond the squad even closer together as their daily training regime intensified. The weekend before the next Test, the Lions had two matches, Mick missing the 17-all draw in the 'unofficial fourth Test' against New South Wales on the Saturday but returning to face Monaro at Queanbeyan in a match staged to celebrate the opening of a new £45,000 stand at the country club's ground the following afternoon. He played through the pain barrier, flying straight back to Sydney the next morning with John Ward and Peter Flanagan and missing a regional sightseeing tour after suffering severe stomach cramps. Despite the obvious discomfort, his enthusiasm and quality distribution, which saw Alan Smith claim three touchdowns, saw him named as a substitute for the Second Test at the Sydney Cricket Ground, his versatility value again fast becoming apparent.

With the home supporters eager to see the green and golds wrap up the series and perhaps believing the publicity that the old foe were there for the taking, over 60,000 people turned up, helped by the decision of the Australian authorities not to have the match televised live. By the end the fans were fighting amongst themselves on the notorious 'hill' as a Roger Millward master class, his 20-point haul equalling Lewis Jones' Test match record, saw the Lions home 28-7. A more balanced pack which included Dennis Hartley, Tony Fisher and Jimmy Thompson dominated from the off. Mick entered the fray in the fifty-sixth minute with Great Britain 13-4 ahead; replacing Derek Edwards just as Syd Hynes was also heading for the sidelines after being sent off for retaliation, kicking Arthur Beetson after the big Aussie had taken him high and late. As so often happens when sides are a man down, the remaining players lifted their intensity disproportionately, John Atkinson capitalizing on a Beetson error to set up a storming late rally which caused the Aussie critics to acknowledge that when they played football, the British side was in a different league.

It was a fact not lost on the Australian club sides and while the tourists justifiably celebrated their renaissance, some of them became recruitment targets. Mick's whole approach to both his rugby and life in general made him naturally sought along with fellow Headingley cohorts Syd Hynes, John Atkinson and Barry Seabourne. The Australians loved his no-holds barred involvement, his ability to mix it with the toughest or sting with skill and pace and reports began to filter back to Headingley that he had been made offers from both North Sydney, where Roy Francis was still in charge, and – in the ultimate irony - from the Rabbitoes of South Sydney who were to take out that year's Premiership. The season had begun with talk of Denis Pittard coming to Headingley possibly to take Mick's place, and now Shoey was being courted by his employers. Mick revealed to *Yorkshire Evening Post* reporter John Callaghan on the eve of the Second Test that he had been in unofficial discussions with Souths who had made him 'a big offer' and that he would be prepared to meet them again. Naturally, Loiners Chairman Jack Myerscough was not going to sit back and see his side asset-stripped and when asked about the situation was staunchly defiant to what he regarded as backhanded approaches and rumours. 'If a club has a genuine offer to make, they should, in the first place, approach us officially. In any case, our players were told before they left England that we would not release them to play in Australia and that is still our attitude. We are not so poor that we cannot afford to stand by our principles. Any player emigrating without our clearance is emigrating out of football.' Although that is what Mick is reported to have said he would do, opinion is divided as to whether he would really have wanted to go despite being flattered by the interest. He later told Joe Humphries, 'I would like to play here for a while at least', although according to Barry Seabourne, 'A lot of the players were made offers to play for Australian clubs, especially the Leeds lads, but none of us went because we wanted to stay and do more. There was also Headingley, there was no place like it, and the ground was always perfect and fit for a quality side. Back home, Mick knew he was one of a great set of lads.' John Atkinson has a slightly different view, 'A few of us were offered contracts out there and I think we would have all gone if we'd been given the opportunity but Leeds wouldn't let us, they were very strict. Daft as it seems, Mick was probably the biggest home bird of us all but we all talked about it and despite the money being good, we all wanted to test ourselves in that level of competition. It was more a personal pride thing but Leeds said no and that was it – we just said alright.' Leeds secretary Bill Carter confirms that although the prospect of departures was debated, it was never really an issue. 'We heard of the interest from South Sydney in Mick back at Headingley but there was never any official approach from them to the best of my knowledge. He was so impressive over there that it was no wonder clubs were interested in him and wanted him on their books but I'm not so sure he would have gone. He loved his rugby in England too much for that.' Harry Jepson, in contrast, is not so certain. 'Mick loved it in Australia, it was a fantastic place for a young man and I really think that had he had the chance he would have given it a go and he'd have been a sensation down there, another Ned Kelly, he had all the attributes they admired and were looking for in British players at the time. The Aussies had great respect for him.' Ken Eyre agrees, 'Mick ended up playing on the world stage anyway and he would have coped in Australia, he would have revelled in being involved every day in a good climate. You could have put him in any team because of his multi-talents and whatever that side needed he would have provided it, that's how valuable he was.'

By now it was obvious that keeping the Test side together for the Ashes decider was the priority, Mick missing the midweek victories over Western Division and Tommy Bishop's Sydney Colts but a mounting injury toll meant that he was again called upon to play twice in successive days the weekend before the big showdown. The growing confidence of the squad was exemplified against Johnny Raper's Newcastle. A traditionally tough graveyard for touring sides, over 20,000 raucous fans turned up to witness a record mauling of their heroes. Mick began on the bench and was called on at half-time to replace winger Clive Sullivan who had a reoccurrence of hamstring trouble. The Lions narrowly led 17-13 at the time but with a strong wind behind them turned on the style, Mick setting up touchdowns for Bob Irving, Syd Hynes and Peter Flanagan in concert with strong running back-rower Phil Lowe. The *Sydney Morning Herald* acknowledged that the 'Englishmen' were 'Too big, too fast and too knowledgeable in their unprecedented thrashing. Dennis Hartley, Phil Lowe, Doug Laughton, "Flash" Flanagan, Keith Hepworth, Alan Hardisty, Chris Hesketh, Mick Shoebottom – these are but a few of the visitors who left the Newcastle defence standing.' Coach Whiteley said that he was thrilled by the 49-16 success and that for the first time on tour his side had really expressed themselves against top class opposition. He was less happy with the tactics of Riverina at Wagga Wagga the next day, Mick producing his usual grafting stint from scrum-half in a 12-11 success as the hosts tried everything they could to injure and disrupt any of the Test incumbents for the following Saturday. In the event, there was only one change to the Lions line-up, at full-back. Derek Edwards and Ray Dutton were already ruled out through injury and it seemed as though Bradford's Terry Price would recapture his First Test spot despite receiving the most savage of the criticism for his display in Brisbane, but a mysterious fever contracted at Wagga ruled him out of contention. After the match, in which he kicked three vital goals, the former Welsh rugby union international complained of a cold but as the week wore on the virus affected his muscles, leaving him shivering in bed and eventually diagnosed with a slipped disc which limited options for the GB management. On the Thursday, manager Jack Harding accepted the inevitable and quietly informed Shoey that he would be taking over although the official announcement would not be made until just before kick-off to keep the Aussies guessing. Mick's reaction to the news that he would be playing in an unfamiliar role in the most important representative match in a player's career was typically upbeat. 'It couldn't have been more than about eight times, but I don't mind playing in the number one shirt one bit.' He told the *Daily Mirror*'s Joe Humphries. 'Anyway I don't mind where I play so long as I get a game and a chance to take a crack at the Aussies.' It was expected that once the hosts got to know that he was the last line they would pepper him with kicks but, as Humphries reported, the British management had no concerns on that score, 'He is a rugged enough player to discourage the Aussies from trying exploitation tactics with long raking kicks.' John Whiteley added, 'The beauty of this side is we have no single stars – they are all good. And if one has a bad patch it won't throw the other thirteen out of gear. We must play football not fisticuffs, fighting wins nothing. I have impressed upon my players that they must keep out of trouble even if it means turning the other cheek, until we get the game tied up and won.' The Aussies had injury problems of their own, selecting four new caps and a major surprise at full-back with Eastern Suburbs' Alan McKean selected purely for his goal kicking with Langlands still out, and future legend Bobby Fulton appearing in the centre. It appeared that their tactics were to remain in contention long enough for McKean to kick them to victory and it was a strategy that so nearly worked. Interest in the decider was enormous, with fans queuing overnight to gain a vantage point, as downtown Sydney was brought to a standstill. If anyone personified the battling qualities of the tourists in the most intense and intimidating atmosphere, it was Mick. The more the Aussies kicked to him, the greater he relished running the ball back at them and that confidence radiated throughout a side that was always on top but never clear. Penalty concessions had been a constant worry and referee Don Lancashire gave the hosts a two-to-one advantage throughout a feisty contest which kept them in it, McKean doing the job he was brought in for with seven successes out of eight. Had that been enough to win, it would have been one of the greatest injustices in the sport's history, Britain scoring five tries to one, the clincher coming two minutes from time when Roger Millward crossed in the corner. John Atkinson sums up the feelings of the British players that fateful day. 'McKean kicked four penalties out of the same piece of sand and Bob McCarthy scored their only try when he was miles offside. Mick had been uncomfortable at centre and he'd struggled a bit at stand-off because he played too much like the Australians' style of play but when he moved to full-back and he could come into broken play where he liked, he thought it was brilliant and he was. I remember lining up for the national anthems just before the Third Test and the Aussies looked like gods in their green and gold, all a bit tanned. I looked down at our lot and their two at five-foot-four, Roger and Keith, all a bit white – we hadn't even got any tan at all – with our white shirts we looked terrible, like we should be in hospital. All I could think was "what am I doing here?", then I saw Shoey and I knew I'd be alright as he would be behind me. He was always shouting at you, encouraging, he never stopped talking when he passed you. You needed him to be on tour not only because of the way he played rugby but because of the way he was, he always kept your spirits up.' Arthur Haddock relayed, 'Millward was again one of the heroes of Britain's victory – along with his half-back partner Hepworth, loose forward Reilly, second rower Laughton and full-back Shoebottom.' Mick's best moment came early in the second half with the Lions 15-12 ahead. 'Shoebottom revealed again Britain's far better attacking ideas and shot through, off Reilly and Millward, to make a second try for Atkinson', noted Haddock while Eddie Waring in the *Sunday Mirror* said, 'Shoebottom made a brilliant attacking burst, Atkinson was up in support to score a fourth try.' It broke the Australians' resistance, especially when Beetson was sent off on the hour for upper-cutting Cliff Watson, having already broken Hynes' nose. In the closing stages, Mick's was one of three drop goal attempts to just sail wide of the posts before Bob McCarthy's chase of a loose ball four minutes from time astoundingly put the Aussies only a point behind. McKean's only miss from the touchline kept Great Britain just ahead and Millward's dramatic late dash, beating four pursuers, brought justice. Eddie Waring added, 'It was a tactical as well as a technical triumph for the tourists. Shoebottom settled down splendidly in the full-back position, and indeed the entire back division showed much skill and resolution.' Alan Smith

Eddie Waring's match report pays homage to the men who regained the Ashes.

is in full agreement, 'The ground was full and there were not so many English there, maybe a thousand poms, and there were oranges coming on the field, cans of beer, and they were really trying to intimidate us. The Aussies had some great players but they'd bombed and pressured out three full-backs during the series and they thought "this is it" when it came to the deciding Test, when it mattered, because we'd put this lad called Shoebottom in. Straight away they started putting the ball up towards him and I could see him with his chest sticking right out before he caught the ball and that just gave him and us so much confidence. You don't realize at the time how much winning the Ashes means and what you've done, that has become more significant as time has gone on, there was another game the next day and we all just wanted to play. We'd get strapped up here and there and be off again and warm to the task. Shoey would have been the first to celebrate though in the bath afterwards.'

For manager Jack Harding, it was one of the greatest days for the British game. 'We beat the Australians and the referee and touch judges who tried to give them all the penalty goal chances they could', he said. After being mobbed on their lap of honour with the Ashes trophy, the Lions were joined in their champagne-soaked dressing room by Bobby Charlton who was in the country running a soccer school. 'The scoreline looks ridiculous – there was only one side in it as far as football was concerned', he ventured. 'What a great match. What a great win!' Even the Australians, who had delighted in rubbishing the tourists after their insipid showing in the First Test, were full of praise. Respected journalist Ian Heads noted in the *Sydney Morning Herald*, 'The Englishmen [*sic*] gave Australia an eighty minute lesson in the skills of rugby league football.' Barry Seabourne is convinced that the media over there unwittingly helped. 'We gradually built up an understanding and drew the series back to a decider but the daftest thing the Aussie press could have done was to write us off. That gee'd us up even more to prove them wrong and the Third Test was a lot more convincing than the scoreline and immensely satisfying.' Australian coach Arthur Summons proclaimed, 'There can be no complaints. Although we had chances to win, they were clearly the better side. With their young, talented players coming along, they could hold the Ashes for many years.' There was further reason for the British players to congratulate themselves, the excellent gates for the Tests ensuring that their 35 per cent stake in any profits generated would guarantee a substantial bonus. Doug Laughton took the official Man of the Match award in the decider but he is eager to pay tribute to Mick's overall contribution to the Ashes success. 'On tour he was always full of fun and liable to play practical jokes; you couldn't take your eyes off him for a minute without wondering if he was up to something, which is ideal in a touring squad. He was always bubbly; I don't ever remember seeing him down or saying that he was homesick like some of the other lads did. He just wanted to get on with it and every day was like a new challenge to him. I don't think we would have won the Ashes series in 1970 without him. We were really struggling for a full-back but he did a tremendous job there on defence and attack. That taught me that you don't have to be a specialist, or to play in a particular position if you are a great player. I would have to give him or Roger Millward the Man of the Match in the deciding Test. If there is one word to sum Shoey up it would be effervescent.' Alan Hardisty, who captained the mid-week side, concurred. 'I was grateful that the tour to Australia turned me from a playing "enemy" of Mick's into a very good friend. He was the type of player you must have if you are going to win trophies. He was the most professional player I ever knew.'

Despite justifiably raucous celebrations that lasted well into the early hours for most, and beyond for some, there was the final match of the Australian leg to complete the following afternoon. John Atkinson laughs at the instructions from the British management post match. 'After the win Johnny said, "I don't care what you do but I need you in the foyer tomorrow morning", so that he could pick a side for the game that day. The celebrations began in the dressing room and that feeling was the highlight of everything; we'd won the Ashes on Sydney Cricket Ground and I'd scored tries in two of the Tests. I felt like it couldn't get any better than that and I guess it never did. There was a big fridge in the corner and it was full of bottles of beer so we started there. We went back to the hotel, got changed and went out into Sydney and it was brilliant. There was no animosity even though the Aussies had been desperate to win and there was massive interest in us so we stayed out all night. The next morning the last thing we needed was a long coach drive but we were desperate to win to keep the record going and we somehow managed a narrow victory. We drove straight back, packed and got a 6 a.m. flight to New Zealand the following morning so we hardly had time to take in winning the series.' Again there was no question that Mick would not be heavily involved and he duly delivered a try from full-back in an easy 24-11 success over Southern Division at Woollongong.

Intensity after such a momentous, hard-fought series inevitably flagged once the tourists headed out for the second leg despite a telegram from RLHQ at Chapeltown Road which read, 'Congratulations on a wonderful record in Australia, please repeat in New Zealand', awaiting them on their arrival in Auckland. Gone were the baked pitches and sun, replaced by quagmires and driving rain as the Lions faced seven more matches in three weeks including

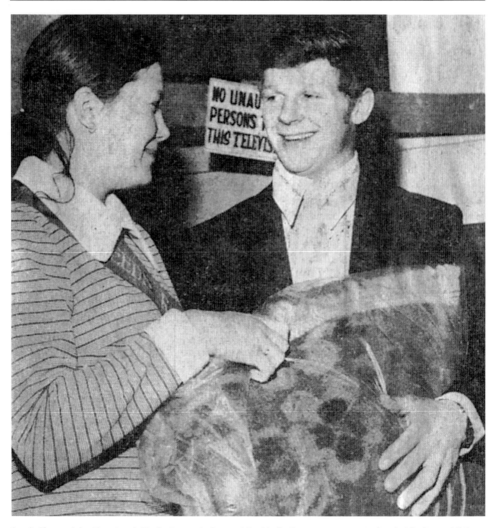

Leeds Player of the Year. Leeds Rugby League's Queen Miss Linda Capper presents an electric blanket to Mick Shoebottom to mark his selection as the Leeds Supporters' Player of the Year in the 1969/70 season. The presentation was made at the Headingley Social Club.

three Tests. The opening one was six days after their arrival with Mick again at full-back in a narrow 19-15 win, complacency nearly wrecking the squad's renewed aim of going through this leg unbeaten. Three days later against a Wellington XIII, Mick moved to centre, scoring one of fourteen tries – Alan Smith getting five and John Atkinson three of the others – as the hosts were taken apart 60-8 on a pitch reminiscent of the 1968 Cup Final at Wembley. Although the opposition posed little threat, coach Johnny Whiteley still rated the performance, calling it 'out of this world' as his charges gave full vent to their ball handling abilities. Widnes' full-back Ray Dutton returned from injury for the second encounter with the Kiwis, in Christchurch, as the British management elected for a policy of giving every player in the squad the taste of Test match football, Mick making way. His final appearance came in his favoured stand-off position against West Coast in Greymouth in another big win which this time saw Syd Hynes claim four touchdowns. In completing the New Zealand leg undefeated, the 1970 Lions came home as the most successful tourists ever to leave these shores with just one defeat and one draw from their twenty-four matches. It left Manager Jack Harding a proud man. 'This has been an exceptional tour', he told the gathered reporters at Manchester airport on their return. 'We have had complete harmony on and off the field.' He was later to add, 'To have a successful tour one not only has to have great players but also great gentlemen, and Mick Shoebottom was both of these. He was one of the outstanding personalities of the tour and his ready wit, which would have done justice to "The Comedians" made sure that the spirit of the party was always very high.' His sentiments are still echoed by captain of that historic outfit, Frank Myler. 'We had seven or eight great players in the team but it was two unsung heroes from the tour that had a big bearing on the outcome of the Tests. Jimmy Thompson wasn't really expected to get into the team but he played in the Second and Third Test matches and was a tower of strength and then there was Mick Shoebottom. He played centre, stand-off and full-back – wherever he was needed, that just summed up what we were about. It was Mick who made the crucial break in the Ashes decider.' Coach Johnny Whiteley's comments followed the same theme. 'When people talk about professionals they conjure up visions of players to whom training and playing is something of a bore. It wasn't a bore to Mick, he fairly bubbled with enthusiasm and joy when he had a rugby ball in his hands, whether it was at a training session, one of our local grounds, Sydney Cricket Ground or Wembley. He loved to be involved and his contribution to the success of the tourists was considerable, on and off the field. The wonderful team spirit of the side revolved around the fun and humour of Mike, he always played with a wonderful cavalier style and a smile.' It was also something that gave Mick intense personal gratification, as he related to Leeds Secretary Bill Carter on his return. 'He absolutely loved representing Great Britain and was very proud whenever he was selected. He appreciated being recognized for what he did but he was never boastful. Being an international justified the effort he put into the game, he never saw it as offering any kind of enhanced status amongst his team-mates. I went out for a drink with him not long after he had returned from the Ashes tour and all he kept saying was how pleased he was that all the Leeds lads had done well for their country and how the team had given the supporters something to cheer and remember. He always had a great affinity with the fans.'

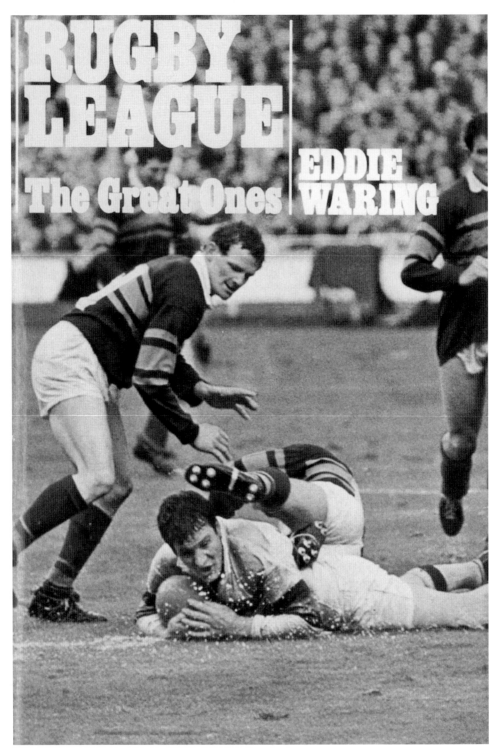

A typically flamboyant try, against Hunslet at Parkside in October 1967, sums up Mick's passion for his profession.

9

1970/71
PEERLESS BEST

Although the potential for burnout after such a strenuous summer was a principal concern for all the tourists and their welcoming clubs, there was a huge incentive for the squad to stay fit and in form with another World Cup on the immediate horizon. Only two years after Mick had suffered the disappointment of missing out on reaching the Final in Australia, he had the perfect opportunity to set the record straight as the 1970 tournament came to the north of England with the showdown decider earmarked for Headingley. The bulk of the Ashes victors were expected to retain their places for the two-and-a-half week festival in late October and early November, but the quality of half-backs around meant that there could be no let up in the fervent Shoebottom training regime. Just over two weeks after returning from New Zealand, Mick took his place – along with his four fellow tourists – in the Leeds side that contested the Lazenby Cup at Hunslet, scoring a try in a comfortable if bruising victory. Two comprehensive wins in five days opened the Championship campaign, with Mick partnering local youngster Chris Fawdington as Featherstone and Widnes were overrun. A typical, mazy run to completely bamboozle the Chemics defence and set up John Atkinson for the first of his three tries was a highlight of the opening home game of the campaign. Eddie Waring said of his form, 'Leeds fans must have been relieved to see that the tour has not knocked any of the shine off their favourite. Indeed, in the two matches I have seen him Shoey looked, if anything, faster and just as powerful. The way he burst through and scorched 50 yards or so in setting up tries for Atkinson against Widnes and Hull Kingston Rovers was stand-off play at its brilliant best.' Atkinson found that getting back into the groove quickly dispelled any overriding thoughts of exhaustion. 'Returning to winning ways at Headingley straight afterwards said more about the side and the pattern of play than individuals. In the first home game, against Widnes, all five Leeds lads and Ray Dutton had paraded the Ashes trophy round the ground and I got a hat-trick down the South Stand side which my dad reckoned were the best tries he'd seen. After the last one I can remember thinking, "jeez, this is easy" and I think it was Alan (Smith) who said on his return that he suddenly thought that he could do anything and Mick was the same. We were fit, we'd trained every day, we were on the top of our game – I think I was as fast as I'd ever been, something like 10.6 for the hundred which would have got me in the Olympic team at the time – but eventually the mental side got to us a little bit, we'd played an awful lot of rugby. We had such a good side though, that we all complemented each other.'

The early rounds of the Yorkshire Cup were completed prior to the World Cup commencing with the Final scheduled to come after the international extravaganza, two months later. Leeds were given a tough draw at the first hurdle, away at Wakefield who they had not beaten at Belle Vue for ten seasons. The tie was on a knife edge at 5-5 in the fifty-fifth minute when Mick's dynamic burst, in concert with John Langley, set the position for Bob Haigh to crash over against his former club and set up a merited win. There was little better luck with the velvet bag and balls in the second round, the severely depleted Loiners being sent to Castleford where the crowd of nearly 12,500 gave them little chance. A young pack containing teenage props Alan Bence and Steve Pitchford more than held their own in a typically robust first half while Mick took over in the second, supporting a break by Syd Hynes and carried on by John Holmes for the match-winning score. An overcrowded schedule to accommodate the World Cup meant that the Castleford match was his second in a punishing spell of five games in ten days which included playing at centre for Yorkshire against Cumberland at Whitehaven. It was a match of immense significance for Shoey not because of its relative importance in the Rugby League calendar but because he was honoured and humble to be appointed to captain his county. Despite helping set up a try for Jimmy

Some of the British players selected for the 1970 World Cup tournament smile for the camera at Headingley. Mick, in the middle, had more reason to than most having just been passed fit to participate.

Thompson, the White Rose went down 21-15 but Mick, much to his relief, had done enough to gain selection for the nineteen-man World Cup squad. A fine try-scoring performance at Batley, the first of another clutch of five fixtures in ten days, where he was 'by far the most penetrative Leeds back' according to Arthur Haddock, was the perfect preparation for the Yorkshire Cup semi-final against Hull. For the vast majority of the clash it looked as though Leeds would suffer their usual Boulevard fate but sheer will and tenacity kept them in a contest they dramatically snatched in the final minute by a point. *Yorkshire Evening Post* reporter Trevor Watson was in no doubt as to who led the larceny. 'Shoebottom, tigerish as ever, was the man to drag Leeds through. He took the game by the scruff of the neck as Leeds went 6 points in arrears after forty-four minutes. His brave running and fearless tackling, with help from Fawdington, cut Hull's effectiveness. He ended with a hand in both tries, a drop goal and an incredible amount of work to his credit.'

He resumed his half-back partnership with Barry Seabourne, who was playing his first game of the campaign after picking up a serious thigh injury on the Ashes tour, at Wigan, scoring another superb solo touchdown in defeat but picking up a back injury himself, which saw him miss the next three Leeds matches in the run up to Great Britain's opening World Cup clash against the Australians, also at Headingley. Along with Malcolm Reilly, who had just returned after a significant lay-off, Mick faced one of the most gruelling fitness tests of his career when the squad met up for their first training session in Leeds in the week leading up to the Ashes re-match. Team manager Jack Harding arrived saying, 'If anyone is at all doubtful he will have to be replaced. We just cannot take any risks.' Shoey was the only one of the party not to have played some part in a game in the previous seven days but, relishing the arduous check over, he showed little sign of concern. 'They can hit me with a sledgehammer if they want', he said. 'I feel champion. I trained last night without any trouble and I'll do anything they want me to.' The Aussies opened the tournament with a comfortable nine-try midweek win over New Zealand at Wigan to show their intent, their coach Harry Bath commenting afterwards that he was delighted Great Britain would be going in without broken leg victim Roger Millward who had done so much to destroy the green and golds hopes in the summer. Lions skipper Frank Myler was quick to respond commenting, 'Any team would miss a man of his ability but if he thinks Roger is the only danger to his chances then he hasn't seen Mick Shoebottom play stand-off.' Millward was even more bullish about the man earmarked to replace him, giving him a ringing endorsement. 'Our squad looks far too strong but there's another reason why I'm backing Britain – Mick Shoebottom. On tour Mick had to play either full-back or centre and, although he did a fine job for us, his real position is at number six. Now he gets his big chance and I'm sure he is going to give the Australians a real shock. It wouldn't surprise me if he's named the Player of the Tournament.'

The busiest man on the field as the two favourites met in their quest for the newly commissioned and sponsored 'Vehicle & General Trophy' was referee Fred Lindop. The match was always going to be a trial of strength and the near 16,000 fans were gripped by the ferocity and intensity of it as two players were booked and four cautioned. One of those who found his name lodged with the man in the middle was Australian full-back Eric Simms, whose late challenge on Mick allowed Ray Dutton to kick Britain's only points of the first half in reply to two drop goals which had given the visitors a narrow lead with a strong wind at their backs. A typical flying tackle at the start of the second half saw Mick deny former

GREAT BRITAIN WORLD CUP TEAM — 1970

Photo reproduced by courtesy of The Yorkshire Evening Post

Back row (left to right): R. Dutton (Widnes), J. Thompson (Featherstone Rovers), D. Laughton (Wigan), D. Hartley (Castleford), C. Watson (St. Helens).
Centre (left to right): R. Haigh (Leeds), C. Hesketh (Salford), M. Shoebottom (Leeds), A. Smith (Leeds), M. Reilly (Castleford), D. Chisnall (Leigh), A. Fisher (Bradford Northern), J. Atkinson (Leeds).
Front row (left to right): K. Jones (Wigan), K. Hepworth (Castleford), F. Myler (St. Helens), S. Hynes (Leeds), P. Charlton (Salford), K. Ashcroft (Leigh).

Above: Great Britain World Cup Team 1970. From left to right, back row: R. Dutton, J. Thompson, D. Laughton, D. Hartley, C. Watson. Middle row: R. Haigh, C. Hesketh, M. Shoebottom, A. Smith, M. Reilly, D. Chisnall, A. Fisher, J. Atkinson. Front row: K. Jones, K. Hepworth, F. Myler, S. Hynes, P. Charlton, K. Ashcroft.

Opposite: Great Britain 11 Australia 4 at Headingley in the round robin phase of the 1970 World Cup.

Bradford winger Lionel Williamson and he was instrumental in gaining the position for Dutton to level with another penalty soon after, leading a charge which Syd Hynes and Keith Hepworth continued. The defining moment, and only try, came when Hynes scorched over after superb interplay by the British pack, Mick being famously caught on camera in all the Sunday newspapers leaping for joy behind his close friend and club colleague. Twice before the end Mick broke clear but was just prevented from getting a scoring pass away, once by a fingertip Bobby Fulton knock down, the hosts' eventual 11-4 victory giving them a huge psychological boost. Icy rain in the first full international to be played at Wheldon Road, Castleford, greeted the British and French players the following Wednesday, a try-less match won courtesy of three Dutton penalties with Mick again producing a tireless defensive stint and instigating, along with Hepworth, the few genuine attacking chances on offer. At Swinton the next weekend, the unbeaten Lions eased through to the Final defeating New Zealand 27-17 with Mick gaining more widespread acclaim for a typically energetic display in which he brought the best out of Leeds team-mate Bob Haigh. A shock narrow defeat for the Australians against France at Odsal meant that the other three nations finished on level points, with the Aussies just claiming their place in the anticipated play-off climax for the trophy by virtue of a better points difference. Interest in the Final and the players involved in it was intense and as an interesting aside, Mick's hobbies are listed in the matchday

WORLD CUP HIGHLIGHTS

The British defence wins again and blunts a Kangaroo attack. Mick Shoebottom effects the tackle ably assisted by Malcolm Reilly with Cliff Watson and John Atkinson making doubly sure.

Syd Hynes scores the one and only vital try in the Great Britain-Australia battle. Leeds colleague Mick Shoebottom jumps for joy in the background.

programme as: 'tennis, cricket, chess, cars, classical music and golf'. A couple of those may seem incongruous to the stereotypical image of a Rugby League player but his niece Vicky Parkin confirms that, 'He did like classical music, he didn't have a large collection of records or claim to be any sort of expert but he enjoyed hearing the kind of opera Carol used to perform with the society.' Naturally, the British went into the decider as clear favourites with close on 19,000 fans roaring them on and millions more watching on television. What they witnessed was one of the most unedifying eighty minutes seen on a rugby field with sustained passages of malevolence in a match which became notoriously dubbed as the 'Battle of Leeds'. Animosity between the sides had been building up throughout the close battles of the summer and nerves were heightened when both dressing rooms were hastily cleared before the kick-off after a bomb scare. The Aussies' disappointing run to the Final had seen Harry Bath cancel all their formal engagements in the week leading up to the game and a rigorous training regime undertaken. Although the British tactics received the most criticism, the penalty count of 19-7 in their favour indicates that both sides were culpable in dragging down the reputation of the code. Mick, though clearly adept at handling himself in such circumstances, was one of the victims of an early head shot that clearly reduced his effectiveness. Aussies Eric Simms and belligerent scrum-half Billy Smith received a severe reprimand from referee Lindop but Bobby Fulton and the Australian forwards, especially Bob O'Reilly and skipper Ron Coote, were the more patient amongst the carnage and capitalized on the two chances that came their way. In the first half Coote swept up Malcolm Reilly's dropped pass to send famous footballing-priest Father John Cootes away to put the kangaroos 5-4 ahead at the break and, as the brawling continued, McCarthy's high kick to the left was caught on the full by Lionel Williamson who powered through Mick and John Atkinson's challenge and just made the whitewash. Atkinson scored to put a converted try between the sides but not surprisingly the game ended in controversy with Syd Hynes and Billy Smith sent off and fights breaking out after the final whistle had gone. For Alan Smith, the British players never quite rose to the occasion and failed to deliver their best. 'That World Cup Final was the hardest game I've ever played in and it just built up to a huge brawl at the end near the ramp, but Mick wouldn't have been the guy to start any of it. His natural play was so aggressive but never underhand, he was just such a powerful player. He'd knock opponents down and if they didn't like it well that was the way it was, he didn't have a mean streak in him. We'd just gone off the boil a bit as a team. We'd had this wonderful tour and then after the early rounds, the Final was just one game too many.' While the Australian forwards were rightly lauded for their courage, the British players were left with their reputations sullied after being front page news for all the wrong reasons, the *Daily Mail*'s headline screaming, 'Get these thugs off our TV screens'. Great Britain coach Johnny Whiteley bemoaned, 'We lost all our composure. We even started niggling and that's something we have never gone in for.' Although for Arthur Haddock, 'Even the punching, butting and kicking lacked science. It was crude, much of it done in the open as bitterness prevailed and feuds flared.' Harry Jepson recalls that the game's tarnished image even spread into local politics. 'After that World Cup Final Councillor Ronnie Teeman, a pillar of the Rugby League community throughout his life, proposed to Leeds City Council that headmasters should be instructed to discontinue the sport of Rugby League in schools!' Looking back, John Atkinson has a measure of remorse for the way things worked out. 'I made a public apology to Johnny Raper not long

THE TEAMS

GREAT BRITAIN

Colours:
WHITE JERSEYS WITH RED AND BLUE 'V'

1.	Ray DUTTON (Widnes)	Full Back
2.	Alan SMITH (Leeds)	Right Wing
3.	Syd HYNES (Leeds)	Right Centre
4.	Frank MYLER (St. Helens) (Capt.)	Left Centre
5.	John ATKINSON (Leeds)	Left Wing
6.	Mick SHOEBOTTOM (Leeds)	Out Half
7.	Keith HEPWORTH (Castleford)	Scrum Half
8.	Dennis HARTLEY (Castleford)	Front Row Forward
9.	Tony FISHER (Bradford N.)	Hooker
10.	Cliff WATSON (St. Helens)	Front Row Forward
11.	Jim THOMPSON (Featherstone R.)	Second Row Forward
12.	Doug LAUGHTON (Wigan)	Second Row Forward
13.	Mal REILLY (Castleford)	Loose Forward
14.	Chris HESKETH (Salford)	Substitute
15.	Bob HAIGH (Leeds)	Substitute

The Minister for Sport, The Right Honourable Eldon Griffiths, accompanied by the Director of the Sports Council, Mr. Walter Winterbottom, O.B.E., will be shaking hands with the teams before the game.

Forty minutes' play in each half. Ten-minute interval. If the game results in a draw, the replay will be at St. Helens on Monday the 9th November, kick-off 7.30 p.m. Turnstiles open.

Music before the game and at half-time will be played by the Leeds City Police Band, by courtesy of the Chief Constable, Mr. A. Angus.

AUSTRALIA

Colours:
DARK GREEN JERSEYS WITH YELLOW 'V'

1.	Eric SIMMS (South Sydney)	Full Back
2.	Lionel WILLIAMSON (South Sydney)	Right Wing
3.	John COOTES (Newcastle)	Right Centre
4.	Paul SAIT (South Sydney)	Left Centre
5.	Mark HARRIS (Eastern Suburbs)	Left Wing
6.	Bob FULTON (Manly-Warringah)	Out Half
7.	Billy SMITH (St. George)	Scrum Half
8.	John O'NEILL (South Sydney)	Front Row Forward
9.	Gary TURNER (Newtown)	Hooker
10.	Bob O'REILLY (Parramatta)	Front Row Forward
11.	Bob McCARTHY (South Sydney)	Second Row Forward
12.	Ron COSTELLO (Canterbury)	Second Row Forward
13.	Ron COOTE (South Sydney) (Capt.)	Loose Forward
14.	Ray BRANNIGHAN (South Sydney)	Substitute
15.	Elwyn WALTERS (South Sydney)	Substitute

Referee: G. F. LINDOP (Wakefield)   Touch Judges: J. BRIERLEY (Dewsbury), L. WINGFIELD (Normanton)

Top: Great Britain and Australia 1970 World Cup Final line-ups.

Above: Mick takes a knock that severely restricted his effectiveness in the notorious World Cup Final at Headingley, as referee Fred Lindop talks to Eric Simms and Billy Smith.

Right: The mistimed tackle between Shoey and John Atkinson which saw Lionel Williamson snatch the match-winning try for the Aussies.

135

ago for what happened at the end of that match. To this day I don't really understand why all hell broke loose. I was never the most levelheaded at times throughout my career but I don't really know what went through my mind at the time and why I hit Eric (Simms), I think it might have been a reaction to Mick getting injured. His effectiveness was certainly reduced because when Lionel Williamson scored, Mick and I had lined him up absolutely and he should never have got through but we ended up hitting each other and bouncing off. Mick was coming from in-field and I was chasing back and I can remember thinking, "we've got him, there's no way he's going anywhere" but Mick ended up all over me and that was the difference between winning and losing. We were mentally and physically tired, we'd had a long season, an intense tour, a lot of us had young families – my youngest daughter had been born while I was away – and we were straight back into a new campaign playing two games a week and then the World Cup. By the time we got to the Final we were all a bit jaded and the opening match against the Aussies was the hardest, most physical match I had ever been involved in. The Aussies lost the fight and the match that day but it took a hell of a lot out of us, more than we realized at the time.'

As was so often the case in Mick's career, his ability to bounce back from disappointment, and re-galvanize his team-mates with his infectious dressing room attitude, prevailed. Three days after the World Cup Final he was back in action, this time at scrum-half as Leeds won at Widnes in the second round of the Floodlit Cup, a match which saw his Great Britain cohort Tony Fisher make his Loiners debut. A comfortable win at Warrington in the league preceded the delayed Yorkshire Cup Final against Featherstone at Odsal, with Mick – not one for bravado – unusually predicting a big win beforehand against a side they had thrashed by 50 points just over a month before. 'Cup finals are always hard but while I'm not thinking that we shall get so many points again, I reckon we should get at least twenty', he said. 'The switch to scrum-half doesn't worry me. I admit it's not as good as stand-off but I am ready to play anywhere for Leeds. (Terry) Hudson can go a bit but we won't be standing back and watching him.' His confidence was not misplaced, especially after Rovers' hooker Dennis Morgan was sent off in the twelfth minute, Mick's ceaseless midfield promptings helping to set up a comfortable 23-7 win. Two weeks later and the Loiners qualified for their second shot at silverware, easily disposing of Hull Kingston Rovers at Headingley to reach the Final of the Floodlit competition for the first time. In the run up to the decider against St Helens, Leeds hit peak form scoring 71 points and conceding only 8 points in resounding league wins over Warrington and Whitehaven, Mick's increasingly dynamic partnership with teenage stand-off Tony Wainwright bringing the best out of a rampant back division and Bob Haigh becoming a regular on the try-scoring sheet in what was to become a world record-breaking campaign for the back rower. Consternation preceded the Floodlit showdown when power cuts resulting from Electricity Board industrial action meant that only the BBC television lights were available to illuminate Headingley. Although much of the match was played in ever-lengthening shadows, that failed to detract from an excellent spectacle in which, although defences prospered, there was much sparkling attack to admire. Mick was cleared to play after suffering a blow to the cheek at the Recreation Ground and in a thrilling, high-quality contest, Leeds just hung on to win 9-5 courtesy of a sizzling Syd Hynes try just before half-time to joyously capture the only prize that had eluded the great side of the era.

1970/71

B.B.C.2 TV

FLOODLIT COMPETITION FINAL

OFFICIAL PROGRAMME
6d.

LEEDS
V.
ST. HELENS

on

Tuesday 15th December 1970

at

Headingley Grounds Leeds

Kick-off 7-15 p.m.

The front cover of Floodlit Trophy Final programme.

Mick won a significant personal duel to welcome in 1971 in some style as Leigh were out-played 28-10 at Headingley. Playing opposite the wily Alex Murphy and against a side which had won ten of their last eleven league matches – and had heavily beaten Leeds earlier in the season – he put his mark on the match as early as the fourth minute scoring a wonderful opportunist try when grubbering through, outpacing full-back Stuart Ferguson and hacking on to win the race for the touchdown. Twice he was hauled down just short in lightning raids and his only blemish was when a stray pass was picked off by Rod Tickle who went 65 yards for a try to keep the visitors in touch at the break. His drop goal in the second half put the home train well and truly back on track and former Leeds great Stan Satterthwaite had no hesitation in bestowing the Man of the Match award on him. It was an ebullient performance which brought widespread praise and a further nudge to the International Selectors. Alfred Drewry commented, 'For all his skill, Murphy's impact on the game was not nearly as decisive as Shoebottom's. The main difference was that Shoebottom insisted on thrusting himself into the action at every opportunity. His appetite for work was insatiable, his pace non-stop and his spirit best exemplified by his scoring an audacious solo try.' For John Robinson in the *Sunday People*, Shoey 'was the perfect answer to the menace of Murphy. The Leigh boss spent so much time chasing Shoebottom he rarely had chance to show his own attacking flair.' They were glowing testimonials that were to come back and haunt Leeds fans at the end of the season.

Further representative honours did follow, although few saw his conversion for Yorkshire in a resounding win against Roses' rivals Lancashire as fog enveloped Wheldon Road, Castleford, to such an extent that the 2,000 crowd who braved the elements were let in free. Three days later he engineered a similar outcome at club level as Leeds beat St Helens in another Headingley thriller between the old rivals. In the early stages Jeff Heaton put the visitors ahead and it looked as though it was not going to be Mick's day when soon after he twice slipped tackles in midfield to lay on perfect opportunities for centres Ronnie Cowan and then Les Dyl only for his final ball to miss its intended target. On the hour, his industry paid off, probing for a gap near the Saints line he found Bob Haigh in typical close support and this time produced a majestically timed pass to send the prolific loose forward over. Shoey's drop goal extended a narrow lead and he ensured victory when linking with Syd Hynes to send Alan Smith over for the clinching score. In the run up to the start of the Challenge Cup, a club record six Leeds players were selected for Great Britain for the trip to play the French, the first international since the infamous World Cup decider. Mick earned the tag of being the most versatile international of all time when picked at scrum-half, his fourth back line role for his country in the space of eight months, eclipsing the distinction held by the 1930s French star Max Rousie who played in three different positions in successive internationals. It was an honour he was immensely proud of and in part compensated for the tendency to see him as the perfect cover-all substitute when squads were chosen.

Oldham had no answer to the rampant Loiners in the first round of the Challenge Cup at Headingley, the hosts running in eleven tries for their biggest ever win in the competition. Mick snared one late on and was instrumental in five of the others despite being forced to take a breather early on after taking a heavy knock. It prompted shell-shocked Oldham coach Graham Starkey to comment, 'You've got to admire them. Their work rate is so high they never seem to stop running. They are on the move all the time. Shoebottom epitomizes the Leeds approach. He has played a lot of football in the past two years but he still looks for work. He is the Alan Ball of Rugby League.' That match was his ninety-second in an incredibly hectic eighteen months and Mick gave a dietary insight into his staying power and energy levels when he revealed that he endured one foodless day a week. 'In the normal course of events I like a fair amount of meat and I eat plenty of steak but I believe that it does one's stomach good to have a rest now and again. Therefore one day a week, when I feel inclined, I cut out foods and go over to liquids. I have some fruit juice in the morning and vegetable juices during the rest of the day.' His athleticism and dynamism was even more remarkable considering he had only recently quit smoking, causing him to gain weight. 'I'm not a big eater', he said, 'but since I decided to forego the fags I find myself a bit hungrier.' Misfortune dogged the British side that were defeated 16-8 in Toulouse, from the opening scrum when they lost the services of Leeds rake Tony Fisher who badly strained the ligaments on the inside of his right knee when it caved in around him. Possession from there on in was a rarity for the visitors and within minutes, Mick and new Lions skipper Syd Hynes were vehemently protesting to the referee after Jean Capdouze's drop goal was given despite the Loiners pair claiming it was at least a foot wide of the post. There was even a question mark about the two French tries, Derek Whitehead insisting that he had held up Bonal and Billy Benyon convinced that Serge Marsolan had stepped out of play and back in again when collecting a sliced cross kick. Three days later, Mick was turning out at the Boulevard in the unusual position of centre, as Leeds' club record equalling eighteen-match unbeaten run narrowly came to an end. Against Whitehaven, he received a standing ovation along with fellow international Bob Haigh from the appreciative Headingley crowd when he was substituted just after the hour mark with a big lead already established, Derek Turner resting two of his key men before the looming second round Challenge Cup tie with St Helens. Strong wind bringing driving rain greeted the sides as nearly 17,000 fans cheered relentlessly during that clash in which defences dominated. Mick, from scrum-half set the early lead, courageously holding up second rower Eric Chisnall when he seemed a certain scorer. A scoreless first half only served to heighten the excitement but with the elements now in their favour, Leeds were expected to gain the upper hand. Resolute tackling from Tony Karalius and Kel Coslett in particular ensured Saints remained in contention and with the sides so evenly matched, the longer the clash went on the more it seemed like the first score would prove to be decisive. It came in the fifty-eighth minute, Mick finding space from a pass by Hynes and manoeuvring into position to claim an angled drop goal which sailed serenely between the posts. Five minutes from time, John Holmes did likewise and, despite a desperate Saints rally, Leeds held on to reach the last eight. A week later however, the hero of the cup triumph incurred his coach's wrath as Harry Jepson explains. 'Before a game Mick always used to walk around a lot in the dressing room, he was always on edge. He rarely had a bad game but I can remember a first half at Headingley, against Salford I think, when nothing had gone right for him and Derek Turner was waiting for him in the dressing room. When the players came in Derek normally never used to say a word and they would do what they had to do before sitting down. He always had a pencil in his hand and he used to tap his teeth with it. I knew what he was going to do because he'd said to me on the way in, "Bloody Shoebottom, he might as well be at home", and he launched straight into Mick. "You", he said pointing at Mick with his pencil, "(expletive) Great Britain (expletive) international, you've got ten minutes otherwise I'm (expletive) fetching you off." Well that was the biggest indignity that could ever happen to Michael Shoebottom, to be substituted at Headingley, and straight after the re-start he set up a try and put Leeds on the road to victory, but the two of them really got on well together. Mick carried on a fine tradition in the Headingley dressing room; he was a great practical joker. He was just a lovely hare'em, scare'em lad.' In the cup quarter-final, Leeds faced Bramley in a local derby at a stodgy McLaren Field and despite being clear favourites, never looked like succumbing to the kind of shock that had recently befallen neighbours Leeds United at Colchester – who had a similar record in league and cup over the period. Mick was again in the thick of the action, Neville Haddock summing up his contribution under the headline, 'Mick the Magnificent'. 'It was one of those days when everything happened to Mick Shoebottom in this bruising Rugby League Cup clash', he wrote. 'The Leeds international half-back was a superman with his deadly tackling – and once went in so hard that besides flooring the opponent he also knocked himself out. He also went a bit too far with one tackle and was booked. But Bramley fans, yelling for his blood, no doubt wished he was in their side, especially when Shoebottom's speed and power thrust him past three defenders for the try which made sure Leeds reached the semi-finals.' Man of the Match and a try-scorer in a narrow Championship victory at Widnes, he suffered severely bruised ribs which resulted in his moving to the wing and ultimately withdrawing from the Great Britain side to play France in the return midweek fixture at St Helens. He aggravated the injury against Hull Kingston Rovers the following weekend and was carried off after succumbing in a three man tackle. At the beginning of the week before the cup semi-final clash with arch rivals Castleford at Odsal, Mick looked a real doubt before assuring his legion of worried fans that he would be fit. 'I'm having regular heat treatment and doing some light training… The injury doesn't feel too bad at the moment and I'm confident that I'll be there for the big game', he told Jack Bentley in the *Daily Express*, who described him as being 'as hard as the concrete slabs which he handles at his everyday work'. Mick continued, 'Semi-finals are always hard matches, no matter who your opponents are. In 1969 Castleford had ground advantage. This time we'll be on a neutral ground and all the lads reckon we can do it. We hope the Leeds crowd will get right behind us from the start. Their support is so important in a match like this. When they start to chant all the boys seem to respond. If they do it again on Saturday we won't let them down – I promise them that.' He was as good as his word. A whirlwind start on a glorious afternoon, perfect for running rugby in front of the season's biggest crowd, saw the Loiners 10 points up in as many minutes and they never looked back. Back at scrum-half, his distribution and judicious use of the blind side was key as the Loiners built up a handy 12-4 advantage. Although denied possession in the second half after Tony Fisher went off injured, his interplay with Bill Ramsey and Syd Hynes kept Leeds on the move until his late swivel and dart into the clear and majestic long pass to Ronnie Cowan secured victory and a return to Wembley, amazingly without the side conceding a try in any of the rounds. There was precious time to celebrate with a crucial league match against table-topping rivals Wigan two days later at Headingley. In a tremendous encounter Leeds trailed 10-8 in the final minute when they were awarded a penalty which could have scrambled a draw but they elected to go for the winning try and Ramsey was hauled down a yard short of glory thus ending an incredible fifty-seven match

Castleford loose forward Brian Lockwood is driven into the turf by Tony Wainwright and Mick during the 1971 Challenge Cup semi-final clash at Odsal.

unbeaten home record stretching back to November 1967. That result saw the Riversiders take Leeds' mantle as League Leaders, Mick then featuring in all four wins to finish the regular season as the Loiners ended in third place on the ladder. The highlight was on Easter Monday at Headingley against Batley, when his cleverly disguised pass sent Bob Haigh over for his thirty-seventh try of the season to break the record number of touchdowns in a season by a forward which had been held by Hull's Bob Taylor for forty-five years. During that game Mick caused amusement for the home fans when playing the second half at loose forward after an injury re-shuffle. One loud cry from the stands aimed at him of 'get some pushing

141

done' as a scrum prepared to go down brought a big smile as his resourcefulness and willingness again came to the fore and he responded with another Man of the Match display. Batley were again the opponents a fortnight later in the opening round of the top sixteen play-offs at a rain-sodden Headingley. Leeds won easily, Mick contributing a try after hacking on a loose ball and beating the cover to touch down with an extravagant dive before starting the move which sent in Les Dyl. Salford were next up, and for Shoey a date with destiny.

10

A MUCH BIGGER BATTLE

All that concerned Mick in the run up to the match against Salford was his desire to help his great friend and regular Great Britain roommate Syd Hynes play at Wembley. Dismissed at Wheldon Road for retaliation, along with Castleford hooker Clive Dickinson, Hynes had subsequently been handed a two match ban which would be served prior to the Challenge Cup showdown if the Red Devils were beaten and Leeds made it to the semi-finals of the play-offs the week before Wembley. Mick said the night before the game, 'There'll be no messing about tomorrow. We've got to win for Syd's sake – and we'll do it too. I know we slackened off last time we played Salford, but it won't happen again. If Syd isn't out there with us at Wembley we'll all feel it as much as him. He has been a great captain all season and we all look up to him.' As it turned out, the grievous injury Shoey suffered against Salford meant that not only was he the one to miss the big day but he was also to face the toughest battle of all, for survival. Alan Smith was in the dressing room when Mick was carried in and immediately noticed that this was much more serious than the usual bangs and bruises of battle. 'Ten minutes before I'd tackled Chris Hesketh and ruptured my knee ligaments and was being helped off into the old corner, and I remember it so well, the crowd roared and I stopped hobbling and turned to see this final vision of Mick going on one of his arcing runs from somewhere in centre-field and the defence just couldn't lay a hand on him. He was pulling them in behind him like a comet's tail, they were all trying to get him but he was going straight for the try-line and, of course, everyone stood up and I just saw him squeeze over. What I didn't realize as I was getting treatment in the dressing room was that he was being carried off and how it would turn out. I knew there was something out of the ordinary when they brought him in because his eye was protruding slightly and that was obviously the pressure of the clot building up behind it. He looked terrible and it was a haunting sight. As a sportsman you live a life of optimism, it's in your nature, it's a competitive thing and you all want to win together and so I never thought it would be the end of his career until he had that second operation. I'd never seen Derek Turner cry, he was the hardest man you were ever liable to meet but for him Mick was the complete footballer.' The injury shattered a very special bond, as George Shoebottom confirms. 'Mick thought Roy Francis was great and they got on very well and he was a good mate of "Bucket" Thornett, he went to see him when he was out in Australia, but the man he really related to was Derek Turner. After the incident that finished Mick, Derek said to me, "they could have had anyone else out of the team", he held him in that high regard.' Harry Jepson, as the man responsible for looking after the Alliance side at Headingley by then, was designated by Turner to accompany Mick in the ambulance. 'I vividly remember every minute of the awful afternoon Mick got his injury, it was all so unnecessary. Salford were a good side and they didn't like being beaten. Derek Turner asked me to accompany Shoey to the hospital mainly to find out at that stage if his injury would keep him out of playing at Wembley. I think the houseman in A&E suspected something because he immediately said he would have to call neurosurgeon Myles Gibson in. I didn't realise the extent of Mick's injuries until I said to the examining doctor, "His jaw's broken is it?" He replied, "Yes, but I've a feeling there's more than that." He wouldn't say any more but I had the answer Derek needed. That first week was a terrible time – running backwards and forwards to the hospital.' Bill Carter confirms that behind the scenes the club was very worried. 'We were always conscious of serious injuries to any of our players and at the time of Mick's we were very concerned. It didn't look good from the outset but the feeling that we must do everything to help him recover ran throughout the club. Concussion was always a possibility because of the way he played the game. He went in hard and was always prepared to take the knocks.' Ken Dalby, who was heavily involved at Headingley and became the club's unofficial historian, wrote later, 'Shoey was the eighty-minute all-action man, a workaholic who rarely failed to communicate his zest for the game to the man on the terrace … here was a player who could quicken your pulse and warm the cockles of your heart in deep midwinter. Highly-talented and whole-hearted, fearless and honest, he had always been prepared to sweat blood for whatever team he played. Respected and loved by friend and foe alike…the club, the county, Great Britain, the Rugby League public…all were irreparably the poorer for that one split second of cruel circumstance.'

Despite the obvious mounting concern, the initial prognosis given to the public was more positive, Brian Batty reporting in the *Daily Mail* that Mick had a fighting chance of playing at Wembley and again quoting football chairman Jack Myerscough. 'Shoebottom is still suffering from the effects of concussion and they are going to keep him in hospital for two or three days until the effects wear off. At this stage the jaw is badly bruised and tender, and that is the limit of the damage. Things are looking brighter and at least he is in with a chance of playing in the final.' The Chairman's visit later that week revealed a very different picture, Myerscough saying his confirmed absence 'is a bitter blow for Mick – and for Leeds.' The effect on the team was also palpable as John Atkinson confirms. 'When we lost at Wembley, I don't care what anyone says, it was because we didn't have Shoey. All of a sudden we were having injuries which hadn't happened to us before and we were very aware that Mick probably wouldn't play again. It wasn't an ordinary injury, we knew it was serious and it put a dampener over Wembley, there was something in the back of our minds. We were so much better than Leigh but they took us apart. When he had the second operation we were all so worried about him, there was even some suggestion that he wouldn't survive and we knew his career was over.'

The strain was incredibly hard on Mick's immediate family, with Carol heavily pregnant as he was readmitted for his second and life defining operation. His condition in the immediate aftermath of surgery was satisfactory but so severe that the only way he could appreciate and see his newly-born son was initially by a picture supplied by the *Daily Mail*, Mick's face being shown in the newspaper with a patch over his left eye. 'It's going to be a long job getting

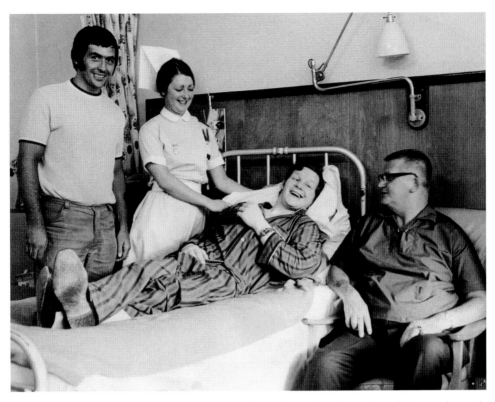

Mick at the start of his long road to partial recovery visited by his brother in the Leeds General Infirmary along with Loiners hooker Peter Dunn (left).

Mick better', said Carol from her own bed in the maternity suite. 'It is something we have to face and accept and now do our best to get him back to health.' Revealingly, she added 'Three years ago when he came back from the World Cup he blacked out and the doctor told him to pack up. But it is a shame that this should happen at the peak of his career. He was over the moon when he came back from Australia after helping Britain to win the Ashes last summer. He always wanted a son, like most sportsmen, and Darren could be a big influence in helping him get better. While Mick has lost his strength at the moment, Darren has taken over. He has got a real Shoebottom grip, big chest, and is like his dad in many ways. But I think it is certain he will never play rugby. Mick said that after he got his injury, and I think we have had enough rugby in the family.'

Nine weeks after his second operation, Mick was allowed home and went on a family holiday but his life was never to be the same again. Specialists told him that it would take between eighteen months and two years for him to return to anything like fitness and although finding speech difficult and suffering from memory lapses, Mick typically declared on his discharge that, 'I'll prove they're wrong. I'll do it quicker than that.' Every weekday he visited the remedial unit at Pinderfields Hospital for speech therapy, writing and spelling classes, but Carol commented that one of the hardest things for him to handle was frustration. 'The biggest problem is that Mick wants to say things but can't explain exactly what it is.

145

A happy group picture of the Shoebottom family at their home in Water Lane, Middlestown, near Wakefield. Mick convalescing after his fight for survival, is with his wife, Carol, four-year-old Amanda and baby Darren.

The Shoebottom family at home. Mick convalescing after his fight for survival, with wife Carol, four-year-old Amanda Jayne and baby Darren.

He knows the word but something stops it from coming out.' Equally, an important aid to Mick's recovery was swimming, and despite having always been a good swimmer he had to relearn from scratch. 'I get very annoyed having to do things slowly and very cross when I can't say what I want to say', he told those who asked how he was coping. His right leg, from which he had initially lost all feeling and movement, gradually returned to normal although it took a lot longer for sensation to come back to his right arm, which affected him being able to write. Vision in his right eye was also severely diminished by the paralysis. Initially, all he could think about before it was formally announced that his career was over was trying to get fit. 'I am just glad to be home. I don't know whether I'll go and watch football or not. It just depends on how I feel', he said. As a result of the turmoil, the domestic environment was a tough one as Mick and Carol had to come to terms with the unexpected changes in their routine and lifestyle. 'Mick's temperament has changed', Carol commented. 'He is moody, gets frustrated quickly at not being able to do things and is sometimes depressed. We don't know how he will be able to cope with the future or what he will be able to do. He is unable to drive, do anything like gardening or help around the house. Before he was placid, now he is less tolerant with Amanda Jayne and Darren. He has less patience and is more quick-tempered. Mick can only eat with a fork, he cannot cut anything. I think he constantly wonders what is going to become of him, whether he will be able to work again and of what he can do, despite making steady improvement.' The strain inevitably told, and the marriage eventually broke up.

His fellow sportsmen clearly empathized with what Mick was going through, their shared passion having been so cruelly denied to him and they queued up in the aftermath to enquire as to his welfare or play a part in his benefit events, his testimonial eventually realizing £20,000 as Harry Jepson recounts. 'His benefit was a tremendous effort which everyone really rallied round to, the bulk of the money being held in trust by the bank for the education of his children. I saw a lot of Mick especially in the early stages afterwards when he was visiting George at his bungalow just off Town Street, in Old Middleton. They used to come over for the afternoon because of the proximity of our houses and it was a heartbreaking sight. I remember my wife Mary, who loved him, saying as they left down the slight slope, "Michael's leading George and he doesn't know where he's going, it's such a terrible tragedy for the two of them and the family." Even in his post-injury period he was such a lovely fellow, he used to ring me up and tell me he'd seen a good player even if he couldn't quite remember for which team or where. He was forlorn at first but then his natural exuberance came to the fore and he was always positive although I don't think he ever really realized how bad his condition was.' Alan Smith, alongside a host of his Leeds comrades tried to ensure that there was an element of inclusion and normality in Mick's social life. 'His mental attitude was always the same, even before the accident, and it made you feel humble in his presence that he did take it all in his stride. He struggled with his speech and movement and we were always helping him but his determination to battle on never left him. He wanted to get into coaching young kids and he never missed a function. He was a great ambassador for the game even after 1 May 1971. The injury changed his life dramatically but he got lots of support, people would pick him up and take him here and there and he really got involved at all levels, whatever the circumstances you could never keep Shoey down. I used to pick him up and drop him home because he lived at Middlestown and I was just up the road and

Mick remained closely involved with the Leeds side wherever possible after his enforced retirement. Here he jokes with long-serving, highly respected kit man Arthur Crowther as the players celebrate winning the 1972 Championship Final against St Helens.

I looked after him. We used to regularly go down to the Star and Garter at Kirkstall after training and on occasions we took Mick with us because we wanted to get him out and were desperate for him to still be a part of the action. Carol used to say, "be careful with him, he's on tablets" but I assured her he'd be alright with us. One night, he stayed up at Headingley with us while we finished our session and then we headed off to the pub. He wanted a pint and he held it in his good hand and then we all got chatting and he must have had a few more drinks than he should have so I took him home. I had this Ford Capri at the time and I laid the front seat back and rolled him in and he almost passed out. Eventually I had to pull over and he was violently sick, I've never seen so much come out of one human being, we must have nearly killed him that night. We got home and I carried him in, much to Carol's chagrin. I don't know if she ever spoke to me again but Mick thought it was absolutely spot-on and the next day he was back for more ringing me up and saying, "Don't forget Smithy, pick me up". He used to get so frustrated because he couldn't get his words out and we always used to try and finish them for him as lads do when you're having a laugh and he used to swear at us but he loved still being involved. We didn't want to patronize someone like Shoey, a man who was so proud, we all just wanted to help him but he knew where he was at and what it was about.' Typical of his determination, Mick gradually fought his way back, getting a job as a warehouseman and then an order checker at a supermarket, 'I am one of only six blokes among thirty women!' he used to joke, even though the pay was less than half what he earned as a sign-writer, blacksmith and player before the injury.

As Mick's recovery hastened, he also took great delight in coaching amateur sides in the Hunslet area where he grew up. The first one was Leeds Sunday League outfit Brassmoulders, based at a pub in Church Street, where he was joined on his debut session in 1975 by *Yorkshire Evening Post* journalist Trevor Watson. 'The Great Britain tracksuit was a shade crumpled but the fact that it was given an airing again meant the owner, former Leeds star Mick Shoebottom, was back in Rugby League action.' He wrote, 'It was the club's first training night for the new season and eighteen players turned up to be given a stiff introduction by Shoey who promptly had them out on roadwork and set the pace on the first lap. Asked what it was like being back in the game even only as a coach, he said: "I'll let you know later." But the old enthusiasm he showed as a player is very much in evidence. He began timing the players on a second lap of the one-and-a-half mile course and was quick to spot that one of his charges had decided to go absent without leave intending to join up with the rest as they came round again. A brisk roasting made it clear that the Brassmoulders' coach had seen it all before and was having none of it. Shoebottom said: "I've had an interest in coaching since I was a youngster and we used to have Bert Cook training us. But as a player you never gave it much thought. A couple of years ago I asked the specialist if I was alright to begin coaching but he advised me to wait. A year ago he cleared me. I watched the side a few times last year and they weren't bad but had one or two raw edges. When I heard they wanted a coach I put in for the job. The main thing now is to get them fit, you can't play this game if you are puffing and blowing. I can show them most exercises but there are one or two I've got to be careful about because of my injury, otherwise I'm OK. I'll see how things go but the way I feel now I'd like to take a proper coaching course. I watched Leeds quite a bit last year and enjoyed it but it is never the same as playing. I suppose coaching is the next best thing and I hope I can make a go of it with Brassmoulders. They've a grand set of lads but they will have

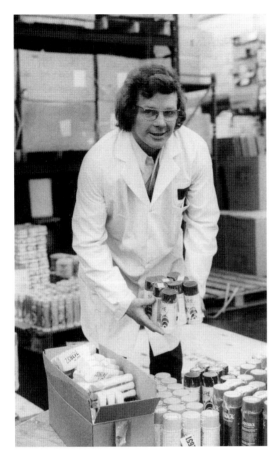

Mick pictured back at work in Makro's warehouse as his rehabilitation continues.

to work hard." The schedule he then drew up for them was certainly daunting, with four-and-a-half miles of road running every Tuesday and Thursday for the first month with only sickness or work accepted as an excuse for not complying and he operated a strict 'no training, no play' policy. Club secretary Stan Cain noted, 'I don't know how the lads will stand up but the committee have accepted Mick's recommendations and the players will – after all it's for their own good.'

Later Mick helped to completely reorganise the Belle Isle club, saying 'We are starting from rock bottom with new facilities, including showers, new strip and, what is more important, new enthusiasm.' But his involvement in coaching was eventually brought to an end by neurosurgeon Myles Gibson who decided that even the slightest accidental physical contact or collision could trigger further brain problems. Mick was always a keen supporter of the Leeds and Lions ex-players associations, doing whatever he could to attend annual dinners and other events as Ray French relates. 'Despite the accident that restricted him, his movement and his life, I never found him to be a bitter man. In fact, rather the opposite, he triumphed over it. He was a great supporter of the Great Britain Lions Association and if he could he would never miss a lunch. Even when he had problems with his speech, he was always there and gave of his best and was highly respected for it. But that summed up his great courage and fighting abilities, he was determined to triumph over it in the end.' Slowly but surely Mick rebuilt his life, liking nothing better than revisiting some of his traditional social haunts. Harry Jepson watched with obvious admiration. 'He worked at Makro for a while, who were one of our early sponsors at Headingley and owned by friends of Jack Myerscough, and at Cooper's on Balm Road just cleaning up and clearing round but neither lasted very long. Mick went back to live with his mother in a council house opposite Coughlan's Field which he eventually bought with his savings and was living in up until he died. He had lots of mates who used to look after him and take him out around the local pubs, the Red Lion at Thwaite Gate run by well-known rugby follower Lol Graham was one of his favourites.' Bob Pickles, Mick's old pal and adversary, was one of his mates and they often met in some of the old south Leeds hostelries. 'After he'd finished I saw quite a lot of Mick around and we used to go for a drink in some of our favourite places in Hunslet all of which had rugby connections. Great friends like Alfie Barron looked after him and took him everywhere but Mick had his good and his bad days.' His highlight used to be going on holiday, leading to a whole fund of new stories and anecdotes, as Ken Eyre recounts. 'Mick got over it, he was never resentful, there were times when he'd forget words or names and click his fingers but you just waited. I never saw him without a collar and tie on or one of his many blazers, he was never scruffy and that said a lot about him and his pride. He had trouble with his hand but he used to go out with the lads, go for a drink in his favourite haunts and had people who he went on holiday with like Paddy and Joe Rainford and Alfie Barron. Shoey coped, he never just shuffled around. Once when he was on holiday somewhere in Spain he either mislaid or lost some travellers cheques so he went to the hotel reception to report it and they put him on the phone to Thomas Cook. The woman at the other end started taking details: which resort he was in, who he had flown with, what hotel he was at and, finally, they asked him his room number. He paused for a while, then said, "Bev Risman, Syd Hynes, Alan Smith." They hadn't a clue what he was talking about but to Mick it was number 132. Another time, when I asked him where he'd been, he said a couple of times, "You know, cricketer, collar", and what he meant was the Shepherd Arms because he could picture the umpire Reverend David Shepherd. Eventually he'd come up with something you'd recognize, you learned very quickly to keep your mouth shut even though you thought you knew where he was going because he did get annoyed if you tried to second guess him. What happened was a tragedy but it didn't crucify him; he had a life. He didn't curl up and die like a lot of people would have done when you look what was taken away from him – maybe another two tours, everything really – but the lad ended up in his own house, doing his own thing and getting help from a lot of friends when he needed it. Nobody could knock him down.' Aside from rugby Mick's other passion was gardening, as niece Vicky Parkin remembers. 'Mick always had green beans on his plate which he had proudly and very successfully grown on his small patch at Midland Garth. His garden was divided in half with vegetables, including beetroot, on one side and flowers and lawn on the other. He never had a bad word to say about anybody and equally wouldn't allow a bad word to be said about anyone when you were in his company. He wouldn't tolerate bad language and just had such a calming nature about him even after everything. Nothing phased him; he accepted and made the best of his lot even right at the end. Whenever I feel down I often think about him and the way he just got on and coped with whatever was in front of him.' Vicky's son Joshua has a special memory of visiting his great uncle. 'What I remember most about him was his smile, and that when we went round he was always eating his dinner.'

In 1999, Mick was honoured as one of Leeds' Millennium Legends, his name appearing with twenty-eight others interwoven into the Rhinos playing kit for that season. After that he was diagnosed with brain cancer but showed typical resilience and fortitude, especially in late summer 2002 when his condition worsened and he was admitted to St James' Hospital. According to Ken Eyre, 'Bill (Ramsey) and I went to see him in hospital just before they moved him to the hospice and although there was no doubt he was dying, he was sat up eating rice pudding and obviously enjoying it. He always had a smile on his face no matter what state he was in and he was never in a way that you could say, "poor Mick" because he was always up for it.' Alan Smith is another to pay tribute to his bravery. 'When I went to see him, even when he was near to the end, it was so, so moving because it just wasn't right for it to happen to someone of such a pleasant nature but he left his mark and a huge impression.' John Atkinson agrees, 'Mick never complained and he never felt sorry for himself; I think we felt more sorry for him. He used to have trouble remembering things and we would always be trying to guess the names of people he was talking about. Right through, and I went to see him in hospital just before he died, he used to hold your hand and just love to recall our feats in Australia or wherever. Even then he was just grateful for what he'd done.'

Shoey was transferred to St Gemma's Hospice in Moortown, Leeds, where he passed away on 12 October 2002 from brain cancer aged fifty-seven. Tributes came flooding in from friends and colleagues, led, not surprisingly, by his former mentor Derek Turner, who was devastated when he received the phone call at work. 'He was half the team', he said. 'He was such a very good player, tackling and attacking. He was a natural footballer and made everyone laugh in the dressing room. He used to get everyone going; he was a real comedian and my right-hand man.' Club, county and country colleague Alan Smith commented, 'He was everything, he had all the attributes you need as a Rugby League player. Everyone who played with him would say he had the lot; he was right up there with David Watkins,

Lewis Jones and Roger Millward. When someone passes on it tends to get exaggerated, how good they were, but not with Mick. He was a smashing lad, with the ball and without it he was a real threat. I have seen him knock forwards back on defence. He was the finest player in a very good squad. I can see him now, in the deciding Test in Sydney in 1970 when the Aussies thought he would be a weakness at full-back; he caught the ball on the run and was just unstoppable.' One of his keenest adversaries in club football and another fellow tourist was Castleford's Malcolm Reilly. 'He was a modern-day player', he ventured. 'He had all the attributes you would want in a Leeds player. He was aggressive, hard-running and with a lot of skill. He was always difficult to play against, there was no quarter given and nothing asked. He was a magnificent tourist; he would have to go down as one of the all-time Leeds greats.' Ray French echoes those sentiments, 'He was a tremendously whole-hearted player and very, very skilful, a beautiful footballer but on top of that he had a toughness, a hardness and just sheer enthusiasm. I played with him a few times and if you walked in a changing room with him he'd be bubbling over, bouncing, laughing and joking and that made him the ideal tourist. He was great for banter on and off the field.'

Bill Carter, who watched every twist, turn and progression of his rugby education, has never forgotten Mick's contribution. 'Even when he first signed as a teenager, there was something about him. During an interview I once did with Radio Leeds they asked me who was the best player that I had seen in my time at Headingley and Michael immediately came to mind. He wasn't the most naturally talented compared to say the likes of Lewis Jones but I admired him because he had such a big heart, was non-stop, always gave his best and was a wonderful character. I think he was the most effective player Leeds have ever had. Personality-wise, I never in all my time there heard him criticize anybody but I heard a lot of Lancashire players bemoaning the fact that he was playing against them, he always seemed to play particularly well against red rose opposition. Names and reputations meant nothing to him. We might have wondered in the beginning about his physique and whether he would be tough enough but he was fearless and always where the boots were flying. He was gifted with tremendous energy and I can't recall, even at the end of some tremendous clashes, that I ever saw him come off the field looking absolutely shattered. He never lost his temper and had such a refreshing attitude to the game because you could always see how much he was enjoying everything. He certainly knew how to look after himself but he never initiated anything, he was hardly ever sent off. He was always near the ball and for me that is the sign of a great player, he was very perceptive. Even though he was so badly afflicted in the aftermath of his injury, in terms of his character he was never one for self pity.' Billy Watts, who has seen all the modern greats come and go at Headingley, is equally unreserved in his praise. 'I think he was one of the best individual players we have had here over the years and as Dougie Laughton used to say after he came back from the tour, "If Mick was in your side, you were okay".' His chief on-field co-tormentor Barry Seabourne has little doubt that the public were cheated out of seeing Shoey make an even greater mark. 'It was desperately sad that his career was cut short, he would undoubtedly have played a lot more international rugby. He was a great player anyway but as the game developed – especially under six tackles – and he would have had more room to work in, he would have been tremendous.' Harry Jepson agrees, 'The sport is a different type of spectacle these days, it's less technical than it was and with the space for players to work in, Mick would have been a sensation under the modern rules, they'd never have stopped him, it was his game.' John Atkinson is in no doubt as to where Mick rates in the pantheon of greats. 'He did everything but he always appreciated the players he had around him. Maybe the sad thing is that I don't think he gets the credit he deserves when they talk about the great stand-off halves. I've played with them all from that era but he was up there with them, he would have transcended any generation. He would have caused mayhem in the modern game; people who watch Leeds now and didn't see him can't imagine his contribution. When he stopped playing it was like there was something missing on a rugby field, we couldn't say, "We're alright, Shoey's here" to whomever we were up against.'

Five days after his death, Mick's funeral and a service of thanksgiving, administered by Leeds Rhinos Chaplin Reverend Steve Mitchell, took place at St Mary's Church in Hunslet where a veritable who's who of Rugby League attended. It was entirely fitting that a man, who had watched him grow up in the district and followed his career as closely as any, Harry Jepson, should give a eulogy. It began, 'This afternoon we are gathered together beneath the spire of this old Victorian church which all my life has symbolized its parish – an area which produced powerful machines of all kinds and dispatched them to all quarters of the world to carry out mighty achievements. We are here to remember a man, to honour a man, to mourn a man and to give thanks for the life cut far too short of a man whose whole being typified the place where he was born and grew up. Michael Shoebottom was power personified on a Rugby League field. Not for him were the niceties of a specialized position. He was simply a Rugby League player. He was a swashbuckler roaming the high seas of the Rugby League pitch. Not only was he quick to spot and exploit to the full any weakness in the opposition's defence but his own was awesome. Sometimes it was strictly clinically effective but at many, many others he was a cross between an octopus and a whirling dervish. But there was more to Michael than just being a great Rugby League player. He had major personal qualities. He grew up during the austerity years after the Second World War and life was never easy for the family. From these difficult circumstances Michael developed and nurtured his tremendous local pride, his courage and his fearlessness. He was always cheerful, even in the dark days, weeks and months following that dreadful May day in 1971. Whenever I asked him how he was he always replied with a smile, "sound as a pound". Even in his late years when he was buffeted by illness, he never complained. I do not wish for a moment to imply that Michael was a paragon – far from it! I remember him as a small fair-haired boy at Low Road School, mischief written all over him. When he made his first appearance for the Hunslet Schools City team at Whitehaven in the annual match against Cumberland in 1958, I wondered if he was ever going to be big enough. Thanks to his days at Bison's in his mid-teen years he did develop wonderfully. A measure of his standing is that when news of his illness reached Australia I was inundated with enquiries and good wishes from the likes of Arthur Beetson, John McDonald, Tommy Bishop and Charlie Renilson. What I am sure about is that, as long as Rugby League Football is played or talked about, the name of Michael Shoebottom will always rank as one who was, both as a man and a player, simply the best.' The other person to speak at the service was long time family friend Ken Eyre who retains the fondest of memories, tinged with sadness. 'It happened to Shoey, it shouldn't have done but it did and I still can't believe another rugby player would want to do something like that on purpose. I wasn't there but I cannot see that being the case.

He was a true eighty-minute player and there were so many instances of him making a crucial break or pulling off a try-saving tackle. Because of the enthusiastic way Mick played the game; his toughness, the way he was involved, the tackling he used to do – it didn't matter how big they were or who they were, sometimes people remember that more but he also had a good football brain.'

A memorial service and burial of Mick's ashes took place at the eastern terrace end of Headingley on 15 November 2002 with a number of his Leeds and Great Britain team-mates,

Mick Shoebottom Memorial-List of Invitees

PETER ASTBURY		FRANK MYLER	
JOHN ATKINSON		PAUL PICKUP	
BOB BATTEN		ALAN PREECE	
JACK BEADNAL		BILL RAMSEY	
TONY BINDER		MALCOLM REILLY	
DREW BROATCH		PETER RENDER	
BILL CARTER		BEV RISMAN	
MICK CLARK		DON ROBINSON	
PHIL COOKSON		KEN ROLLIN	
TONY CROSBY		BARRY SEABOURNE	
ROBIN DEWHURST		ALAN SMITH	
KEVIN DICK		NORMAN SHUTTLEWORTH	
ROY DICKINSON		NOEL STOCKDALE	
LES DYL		DEREK TURNER	
GRAHAM ECCLES		TONY WAINWRIGHT	
ALBERT EYRE		JOE WARHAM	
KEN EYRE		GEOFF WRIGGLESWORTH	
TONY FISHER		PAUL CADDICK	
RAY FRENCH		STEVE BALL	
NEIL HAGUE		PETER HIRST	
BOB HAIGH		CHRIS ROSS	
DEREK HALLAS		SHAUN CALLIGHAN	
ALAN HARDISTY		FAMILY & FRIENDS	20-30
DENIS HARTLEY			
KEITH HEPWORTH		- addresses required	
JOHN HOLMES		BERNARD WATSON	
ALAN HORSFALL		RON COWAN	
ERIC HORSMAN		EDDIE RATCLIFFE	
SYD HYNES		ALFIE BARRON	
HARRY JEPSON		MICK JOYCE	
LEWIS JONES		JOHN BURKE	
JOHN LANGLEY		PETER DUNN	
ROGER MILLWARD			

Memorial list of invitees.

Memorial service and internment of Mick's ashes at Headingley, Friday 15 November 2002. Family and former team-mates gather to pay their last respects as Leeds Rhinos Chief Executive Gary Hetherington presents a specially commissioned portrait, 'Shoey – the Lionheart' to George Shoebottom.

along with a host of fans, present. Elder brother George noted, 'Michael I know would have been proud to witness such a wonderful acknowledgement of his achievements. If ever there was a fitting place for his ashes to be laid to rest, then on the try-line beneath the goal posts at his beloved club was it – rugby was his life.' Even at such a solemn occasion, there was some of the humour that had always been associated with Mick as George recounts. 'His old room-mate "Flash" Flanagan came and sat by me at the do after Mick's ashes had been scattered at Headingley and said, "They wouldn't let me in and I've come from bloody Hull and I had to get two buses" and we had a right session, that was the affect Mick had on people. He said Mick used to drive them all crackers. I was flabbergasted by some of the people I met that day; Jim Mills, Frank Myler, Don Robinson. He and I reminisced about a game I played in against him at Headingley for Hull Kingston Rovers and late on, even though we were losing by a mile, it looked as though I was all on a scorer under the sticks when I got such a bang and this guy knelt on the floor at the side of me and his words were, "Here, have a rest with me sonny"and that was Robbie. You could see how cut up they all were.' Always keenly involved with the Hunslet Club for Boys and Girls which meant so much to him in his formative years, they also ensured he had a permanent memorial. Club Director Danny Webb arranged for a shirt Mick had donated to the club and which had been displayed in a cabinet at their Hillidge Road base to be mounted and framed and put on display at Morrison's supermarket in Church Street for a wider audience. His brother George thinks it is a fine epitaph. 'He donated one of his signed Great Britain jerseys to the club and

I am immensely proud that it hangs in a permanent framed tribute at Morrison's in Hunslet together with an inset action photograph.' Ken Eyre proposed another lasting tribute. 'There is a lot to celebrate and I'm glad I knew him because he brought a lot of joy and laughs into my life. I don't think anybody should forget him and I did ask Gary Hetherington up at the Rhinos to consider retiring the number six shirt, especially since the advent of squad numbers, I think that would have been a fitting tribute and appropriate gesture.'

The final word, significantly, concerns Mick's legacy, as Vicky Parkin reveals. 'Joshua and Samuel, his great nephews, are just starting to train with the junior Rhinos and at Selby Warriors and Josh, in particular, is starting to exhibit some of Mick's qualities – particularly of wanting to do something with the ball every time he gets hold of it. He scored three tries in one of his first games at the Warriors and the coach said to me that he looked a natural stand-off and asked me if there was any pedigree in the family. I just smiled at him and said, "His great uncle could play a bit."'

CAREER STATISTICS

LEEDS (EXCLUDING LAZENBY CUP)

	A	T	G	P
1961/62	4	1	–	3
1962/63	11	3	–	9
1963/64	21	6	–	18
1964/65	25	12	6	48
1965/66	37	8	26	76
1966/67	26	12	10	56
1967/68	44	21	1	65
1968/69	39	18	1	56
1969/70	39	23	2	73
1970/71	42	13	6	51
TOTALS	288	117	52	455

HONOURS

Championship Winner	Leeds v. Castleford	1969
Championship Runner-up	Leeds v. St Helens	1970
Challenge Cup Winner	Leeds v. Wakefield Trinity	1968
Yorkshire Cup Runner-up	Leeds v. Wakefield Trinity	1964
Yorkshire Cup Winner	Leeds v. Castleford	1968
Yorkshire Cup Winner	Leeds v. Featherstone Rovers	1970
Floodlit Trophy Winner	Leeds v. St Helens	1970
European Club Championship Winner	Leeds v. Perpignan	1969

League Leaders' Trophy Winner   1966/67, 1967/68, 1968/69, 1969/70
Yorkshire League Winner   1966/67, 1967/68, 1968/69, 1969/70

GREAT BRITAIN

TEST MATCHES

1968 WORLD CUP:

Great Britain	10	Australia	25	1968	Sydney (centre)
Great Britain	38	New Zealand	14	1968	Sydney (substitute, 1 try)

1969

Great Britain	9	France	13	1969	Toulouse (stand-off)

1970 ASHES TOUR:

Great Britain	15	Australia	37	1970	Brisbane (centre)
Great Britain	28	Australia	7	1970	Sydney (substitute)
Great Britain	21	Australia	17	1970	Sydney (full-back)
Great Britain	19	New Zealand	15	1970	Auckland (full-back)

1970 WORLD CUP:

Great Britain	11	Australia	4	1970	Leeds (stand-off)
Great Britain	6	France	0	1970	Castleford (stand-off)
Great Britain	27	New Zealand	17	1970	Swinton (stand-off)
Great Britain	7	Australia	12	1970	Leeds★ (stand-off)

★Final

1971

Great Britain	8	France	16	1971	Toulouse (scrum-half)

TOTALS: 12 appearances, 1 try
(2 full-back / 2 centre / 5 stand-off / 1 scrum-half / 2 substitute)

OTHER GAMES

1968 PROMOTIONAL MATCHES:

Great Britain	28	Toowoomba	10	1968	(stand-off, 3 goals)
Great Britain	25	North Queensland	2	1968	Townsville (loose forward, 1 try)
Great Britain	33	North West Queensland	5	1968	Mt Isa (substitute, did not play)

1970 TOUR

AUSTRALIA

Great Britain	23	North Queensland	20	1970	Townsville (stand-off, 3 tries)
Great Britain	45	Wide Bay	7	1970	Wondai (centre, 1 try)
Great Britain	37	Toowoomba	13	1970	(scrum-half, 1 try)
Great Britain	34	Monaro	11	1970	Queanbeyan (scrum-half)
Great Britain	49	Newcastle	16	1970	(substitute)
Great Britain	12	Riverina	11	1970	Wagga Wagga (scrum-half)
Great Britain	24	Southern Division	11	1970	Woolongong (full-back, 1 try)

NEW ZEALAND

Great Britain	60	Wellington XIII	8	1970	(centre, 1 try)
Great Britain	57	West Coast	2	1970	Greymouth (stand-off)

TOTALS: 9 appearances, 7 tries
(1 full-back / 2 centre / 2 stand-off / 3 scrum-half / 1 substitute)

YORKSHIRE

Yorkshire	17	Cumberland	17	1966	Workington (stand-off, 1 try)
Yorkshire	17	Lancashire	22	1966	Headingley (stand-off)
Yorkshire	34	Cumberland	23	1967	Castleford (substitute back)
Yorkshire	23	Cumberland	10	1968	Whitehaven (substitute back)
Yorkshire	10	Lancashire	5	1968	Craven Park, Hull (substitute back)
Yorkshire	12	Lancashire	14	1969	Salford (substitute back)
Yorkshire	15	Cumberland	21	1970	Whitehaven (centre)
Yorkshire	32	Lancashire	12	1971	Castleford (scrum-half, 1 goal)

ENGLAND

England	17	Wales	24	1968	Salford (scrum-half)
England	11	France	11	1969	Wigan (substitute)
England	26	Wales	7	1970	Headingley (stand-off, 1 try)
England	9	France	14	1970	Toulouse (stand-off)

Other Rugby League Titles Available from Tempus

07524-2702-4	Barrow Raiders Rugby League Club	Keith Nutter	£10.99
07524-1896-3	Bradford Rugby League	Robert Gate	£10.99
07524-1895-5	Castleford Rugby League	David Smart & Andrew Howard	£11.99
07524-2430-0	Castleford Rugby League Club: 50 Greats	David Smart & Andrew Howard	£12.99
07524-2731-8	Cumberland Rugby League: 100 Greats	Robert Gate	£12.99
07524-3220-6	Don Fox – A Rugby league Legend	Ron Bailey	£12.99
07524-2295-2	Featherstone Rovers Rugby League Club	Ron Bailey	£10.99
07524-1822-X	Headingley Rugby Voices	Phil Caplan	£9.99
07524-2429-7	Hull Rugby League Club: 100 Greats	Raymond Fletcher	£12.00
07524-2957-4	Hull Rugby League Football Club (Classics)	Raymond Fletcher	£12.99
07524-1641-3	Hunslet Rugby League Club	Les Hoole	£9.99
07524-2740-7	Leeds RLFC (Classics)	Peter Smith & Phil Caplan	£12.99
07524-1140-3	Leeds Rugby League Club	Phil Caplan & Les Hoole	£9.99
07524-2225-1	Leeds Rugby League: 100 Greats	Phil Caplan & Les Hoole	£12.00
07524-2693-1	Rugby League Hall of Fame	Robert Gate	£17.99
07524-3087-4	Rugby League in Manchester	Graham Morris	£12.99
07524-3273-7	Rugby League in Wales	Graham Morris	£12.99
07524-1897-1	Salford Rugby League Club	Graham Morris	£9.99
07524-1883-1	St Helen's Rugby League Club	Alex Service	£12.99
07524-2706-7	St Helen's Rugby League FC (Classics)	Alex Service	£12.00
07524-2708-3	Swinton Rugby League Football Club	Stephen Wild	£10.99
07524-1870-X	Warrington Rugby League Club	Eddie Fuller & Gary Slater	£9.99
07524-2299-5	Wigan Rugby League Football Club	Graham Morris	£10.99
07524-2414-9	Warrington RLFC: 100 Greats	Eddie Fuller & Gary Slater	£12.00
07524-3108-0	Wigan RLFC (Classics)	Graham Morris	£12.99
07524-3211-7	Thrum Hallers Halifax Heroes 1945-1998	Robert Gate	£12.99

If you are interested in purchasing other books published by Tempus,
or in case you have difficulty finding any Tempus books in your local bookshop,
you can also place orders directly through our website

www.tempus-publishing.com